BLOSSOMS
IN SNOW

BLOSSOMS
IN SNOW

AUSTRIAN REFUGEE POETS IN MANHATTAN

selected and translated by
JOSHUA PARKER

STUDIES IN CENTRAL EUROPEAN HISTORY CULTURE & LITERATURE
Series Edited by Günter Bischof

UNIVERSITY OF NEW ORLEANS PRESS

Manufactured in the United States of America
ISBN: 978-1-60801-187-2
Copyright © 2020
University of New Orleans Press
2000 Lakeshore Drive
New Orleans, Louisiana 70119

Cover Image: Gottfried Salzmann, *New York, Midtown 1* (2001). Salzburg
Museum, Alpenstraße 75, 5020 Salzburg. © Gottfried Salzmann.
Book and cover design: Alex Dimeff

Library of Congress Cataloging-in-Publication Data

Names: Parker, Joshua, editor.
Title: Blossoms in snow : Austrian refugee poets in Manhattan / selected
    and translated by Joshua Parker.
Description: First edition. | New Orleans, Louisiana : University of New
    Orleans Press, [2020] | Series: Studies in Central European history
    culture & literature | Includes bibliographical references. | Poems in
    German and their English translation.
Identifiers: LCCN 2020006829 (print) | LCCN 2020006830 (ebook) | ISBN
    9781608011872 (paperback ; acid-free paper) | ISBN 9781608011926 (epub)
    | ISBN 9781608011926 (adobe pdf)
Subjects: LCSH: Austrian American poetry (German)--20th
    century--Translations into English. | Exiles' writings, Austrian--New
    York (State)--New York. | Austrian American poetry (German)--Jewish
    authors. | Jewish poetry. | Jews--United States--Poetry. |
    Expatriation--Poetry. | Holocaust, Jewish (1939-1945)--Poetry.
Classification: LCC PT3914.Z5 B58 2020 (print) | LCC PT3914.Z5 (ebook) |
    DDC 811/.609436073--dc23
LC record available at https://lccn.loc.gov/2020006829
LC ebook record available at https://lccn.loc.gov/2020006830

Printed on acid-free paper
First edition

UNIVERSITY OF NEW ORLEANS PRESS
unopress.org

Those fixed on the wandering land: travelers.
Those who flee to the fixed land: the settled.
But those who flee on the wandering land, and those settled on the
fixed land: what to call them ?

J.M.G. Le Clézio, *Le Livre des fuites*

CONTENTS

ACKNOWLEDGMENTS

Thanks to Andreas Kloiber, Ralph Poole, Hannah Rückl, and Karin Wohlgemuth for help with translations and editing. To the Botstiber Institute for Austrian-American Studies for a generous grant supporting research. To the Austrian Academy of Sciences, the Austrian Association for American Studies, Bowling Green State University, SWPS University for Social Sciences and Humanities, and the University of Tampere for an early audience and feedback. I am grateful to Konstantin Kaiser of the Theodor Kramer Gesellschaft, Klemens Renoldner of the Stefan Zweig Centre Salzburg, Veronika Zwerger and Claudia Geringer of Vienna's Exilbibliothek, Christian J. Ebner of the Austrian Cultural Forum, Sarah Painitz of Butler University, Barry Trachtenberg of Wake Forest University, and Günter Bischof of the University of New Orleans and the anonymous reader of the manuscript for their generous time and comments. And to the many family members and publishers who agreed to allow reprintings.

FOREWORD
GÜNTER BISCHOF

"You foreign land, you homeland,
Take me as your son.
Wasn't I already one,
before you knew me?"

Max Roden, "You Foreign Land, oh You Homeland"

On March 13, 1938 Hitler announced the *Anschluss* (annexation) of Austria to the Third Reich from the balcony of the centrally located Imperial Palace on Vienna's *Heldenplatz* (heroes' square) to the world at large. The Nazi *Führer*, born in Austria, was surprised how little resistance his army encountered when the *Wehrmacht* invaded Austria the previous day. What was surprising (to some Germans as well) was the level of meanness and nastiness in the beginning persecution of the Jewish community of Vienna by the local population. Neighbors humiliated and brutalized neighbors and acquaintances. They unleashed "wild aryanizations" – stealing apartments, precious art and jewelry, cars, and eventually villas, factories, theatres and entire businesses. As Philipp Flesch, a refugee to the United States, reported: "Surely never before in the world has been a revolution, when so much was stolen so rapidly and according to plan in an organized fashion."[1] Also

---

1 Philipp Flesch, "Entehrung, Schikane und Mord mit deutscher Gründlich-keit," in: Margarete Limberg/Hubert Rübsaat, eds., *Nach dem "Anschluss"... Berichte österreichischer EmigrantInnen aus dem Archiv der Harvard University* (Vienna: Mandelbaum, 2013), 127-37 (here 133-35).

rarely in the annals of history has a minority been persecuted with such brutal ruthlessness. Starting on the nights of March 11 and 12, when the *Anschluss* was politically effected, Viennese Nazis came out of the woodwork and organized "scrub squads" with their Jewish neighbors. Jewish men and women were taken from their homes and forced to clean the streets on their knees. They were brought to Nazi barracks where they were forced to scrub floors and toilets and also physically exercise until they collapsed. Doctors were spared, but lawyers were considered "particularly suitable material for scrub squads." And so were rabbis. Vienna became a model for Nazi persecutions of Jewish neighbors in the Third Reich.[2] Or, as Albert Ehrenstein put it in his poem "Emigrantenlied": "Dann sind die braunen Wuthunde gekommen."

Few Austrian Jews had left Vienna, prior of the *Anschluss*. Like German Jews they did not see the handwriting on the wall when Hitler's Germany began persecution of Jews with the Nuremberg Laws of 1934. After the *Anschluss* most Jews tried to leave the *Donau- und Alpengaue*/the *Ostmark*—the Third Reich's new geographic designation for Austria. Not all could afford to leave. Where to go? Essentially, wherever they could get immigration papers. You could get into Shanghai without a visa; thousands went there. They left for Australia and Latin American countries. Many went to Palestine, still under British occupation. Others left for Great Britain, Sweden, Czechoslovakia, and France. In Prague and in Paris, Nazi invasions soon caught up with them. The French government imprisoned them in internment camps, where life

---

2 Günter Bischof, "Austria's Loss - America's Gain: *Finis Austriae* - The *"Anschluss"* and the Expulsion/Migration of Jewish Austrians to the U.S.," in: Günter Bischof, *Relationships/Beziehungsgeschichten:Austria and the United States in the Twentieth Century* (TRANSATLANTICA 4) (Innsbruck: StudienVerlag 2014), 57-82 (quotation 68); on the *"Anschluss"* see also Manfred Flügge, *Stadt ohne Seele:Wien 1938* (Berlin: Aufbau Verlag, 2018), and the "Roundtable" on the book in Günter Bischof/David M. Wineroither, eds., *Democracy in Austria* (Contemporary Austrian Studies [CAS] 28) (New Orleans-Innsbruck: UNO Press/Innsbruck University Press, 2019), 275-305.

was mostly miserable. The British government interned German and Austrian refugees (Jews included) on the Isle of Man. Exiles and Americans initiated an "Emergency Rescue Committee" in New York in 1940. They collected funds and sent the refugee helper Varian Fry to Marseilles to "save" well-known Central European artists and scholars (many of them Jews).[3] Individuals like Josef Buttinger, a former young leader of the Revolutionary Socialists, himself a stateless refugee in France, was interned for many weeks in a miserable French camp. Married to the wealthy American Muriel Gardiner, Buttinger managed to get out and make it to New York with his wife, where the two of them became "refugee helpers." They assisted numerous Austrian Jewish and Socialist regfugees with affidavits and funds to make it to the United States and even rented apartments for the newcomers and put some of their children through college.[4] The Nazis not only persecuted Jews but all their political opponents—Socialists, Communists, and Austrian Fascists.

Most of the poets and writers presented in this unique collection edited and translated by Joshua Parker were refugees from Vienna (and Prague and places further east like

3 Anne Klein, "Politische Verantwortung in Krisenzeiten: Transatlantische und lokale Asylnetzwerke des österreichischen Exils, 1940-1942," in: Evelyn Adunka/Primavera Driesen-Gruber/Simon Usaty with Fritz Hausjell and Irene Nawrocka, eds., Exilforschung: Österreich. Leistungen, Defizite & Perspektiven (Exilforschung heute vol. 4) (Vienna: Mandelbaum Verlag 2018), 459-78 (here 460-61).

4 Günter Bischof, "Busy with Refugee Work." Joseph Buttinger, Muriel Gardiner, and the Saving of Austrian Refugees, 1940–1941, in: Zeithistoriker – Archivar – Aufklärer: Festschrift für Winfried R. Garscha, ed. Claudia Kuretsidis-Haider and Christine Schindler im Auftrag des Dokumentationsarchivs des österreichischen Widerstandes und der Zentralen österreichischen Forschungsstelle Nachkriegsjustiz (Vienna 2017), 115-26; Philipp Strobl, "Thinking Cosmopolitan or How Joseph Became Joe Buttinger," in: Günter Bischof/Fritz Plasser/Eva Maltschnig, eds., Austrian Lives (CAS 21) (New Orleans/Innsbruck: UNO University Press-Innsbruck University Press, 2012), 92-122; Klein, "Politische Verantwortung," 461-64.

Czernowitz). As stateless refugees they struggled to get out of Hitler's *Ostmark*. They faced the same obstacles as thousands of others who tried to get visas to come to the United States. Their routes to the US via France, Spain, Portugal, Great Britain, and other places were as varied as those of all refugees of this era. With his cameo life sketches of each of the poets and writers featured in this collection, Parker provides us with basic background information where they came from, how they got to the US, and what became of them in America. They faced the strict American immigration laws, which also had an anti-Semitic spin. The quota laws of 1921 and 1924 were specifically directed against Eastern European Jews and Italians, who had come by the millions in the early twentieth century to become the labor force for the rapidly industrializing United States. There were hundreds of thousands of Galician Jews from the Habsburg Monarchy among these "new" immigrants. With the quota laws nativist Americans aimed at creating a "homogenous" America, favoring traditional "white" Western and Northern European immigrants over "unassimilable" "non-white" Eastern and Southern European immigrants. The 1924 quota for Austrians was limited to a meagre 785 immigrant visas per year. After the *Anschluss* the Austrian quota was integrated into the German quota of 27,370, which was filled in 1939 but not in subsequent years. An 11-year waiting list remained for 300,000 German and Austrian Jews who wanted to come to the United States. Twenty thousand Jews waited in line before the American Consulate in Vienna (downgraded from an embassy). Fewer than a thousand got an interview and thereby a chance to snag a visa.[5] "One isn't born with a passport," noted Berthold Viertel in his poem "Doodle on the Back of a Passport."

Take the story of famed Raul Hilberg, the founding father of Holocaust studies. He left Vienna as a thirteen-year-old with affidavits from his mother's relatives in New York. They got to

5 Bischof, "Austria's Loss—America's Gain," 65-68.

France and managed to get on a boat to Cuba, free but penniless. After four months in Havanna, Raul managed to get a visa to the United States on the German quota. Once he got to New York, he stayed with relatives. His parents, born in Galicia (what would later become Ukraine), had to wait for ten months to get visas on the Polish quota to reach New York and be with their son again.[6] Thus the quota system could break up families, like families are broken up under today's American immigration regime.

The American diplomatic representative in Vienna, John Cooper Wiley, regularly reported Nazi depredations vis-à-vis Vienna's Jews to Washington. On March 25 he wrote:

> There has been a campaign of indignity inflicted upon the Jews. One eminent Rabbi has his beard cut off. Hundreds, if not thousands, have been obliged to perform degrading and menial tasks, and practically all of the Jewish population is in a state of acute anxiety and depression. They feel they were living in a state of *legalized lawlessness* without rights or the possibility of appeal to any higher authority. Suicides have been numerous [my emphasis].[7]

Wiley worked tirelessly to get visas for Jews and even spent his own money to hire more people at the Consulate General (downgraded from an embassy after the *Anschluss*) to process the many applications. Every applicant has to be interviewed to check the validity of affidavits and to make sure that immigrants would not become "Likely Public Charges." In other words friends and family had to support them financially if needed and not the federal government. In the end only 800 applicants were interviewed. Still, an astounding 30,000 Austrian Jews

---

6 Raul Hilberg, *The Politics of Memory"The Journey of a Holocaust Historian* (Chicago: Ivan R. Dee, 1996), 42-47 (here 47).
7 Wiley's dispatch to Secretary of State Hull from March 25, 1938, is cited in Bischof, "Austria's Loss – America's Gain," 67.

found refuge in the United States during the Second World War (27,000-30,000 in Great Britain).[8] In early June Wiley summarized the ongoing crisis to a colleague in Washington:

> The Jews are given no respite. Each time there is a period of calm, it is quickly interrupted. We are in the midst of a new and aggravated wave of Jewish persecutions: wholesale arrests, deportation to Dachau, forced labor in Styria; and the local prisons are overflowing. Every conceivable pressure is being put on Jews to make them abandon their worldly goods and flee the country. There is, I understand a substantial clandestine exodus over the frontier at night. Great numbers appear at the Consulate General with expulsion orders based on "voluntary" acquiescence allowing periods of two weeks or two months for final and definite departure from the Reich. The anxiety of these people is indescribable.[9]

Berthold Viertel observed in his poem "Doodle on the Back of a Passport": "*What's called homeland is now called hell, which you escaped just in time.*"

Suicide was a way out many of the persecuted chose at the time. "Every day one hears of acquaintances that chose death," noted the journalist Rose Marie Papeneck-Akselried. After being tortured by the SA, a well-known doctor took poison with his young wife. The owner of a theater poisoned himself after being beaten almost to death in the streets. A well-known actor cut his wrist after he could no longer stomach "the fury of the brown shirts" (*das Wüten der Braunen*). An actor colleague of his shot his 80-year-old mother

---

8 These are the most reliable figures we have, accumulated by the "Documentation Archives of the Austrian Resistance" (*DÖW*) in Vienna, see Claudia Kuretsidis-Haider, "Exilforschung im DÖW am Beispiel des Projekts 'Vertreibung – Exil – Emigration'," in: Adunka et al, eds., *Exilforschung Österreich*, 621-47 (here 635).
9 Wiley to Messersmith, June 3, 1938, cited in Bischof, "Austria's Loss – America's Gain," 76.

and then himself because he could not emigrate with the sickly old woman.[10] Well-known artists like Egon Friedell committed suicide. There are estimations that 500 people committed suicide per month, probably "several thousand" after the *Anschluss*.[11] We will never know the exact number.

Sigmund Freud left and passed away soon in his London exile. He had cancer and probably was heartbroken. We will never know how many people suffered from "broken hearts." Guido Zernatto, whom the Nazis persecuted because of his affiliation with the Schuschnigg regime, puts it starkly in his poem "This Wind of Foreign Continents": "This wind of foreign continents blows the soul from my body [...] I'm forlorn like a forest animal, crying in winter nights." If we take the homesickness (*Heimweh*) that suffuses the poems published in this volume, almost every refugee suffered from a "broken heart." The many soulful references to their native Vienna pervade these pages, as does their desire and strong will to find a new home in their American exile.[12] Egon Frey put it this way in his poem "When Darkness Threatens…": "Where does the soul fly when darkness threatens? To you, memories." And Gertrude Urzidil in "Great Skill": "A part of the heart stayed behind in Prague, in America I'm just travelling." And Max Roden again in "House of My Homeland": "Echo-wall of footsteps. House of my homeland. I've left you behind me, my footsteps ring hollow."

New Orleans, September 2019

---

10 Rose Marie Papenek-Akselried, in: Limberg/Rübsaat, eds., *Nach dem "Anschluss,"* 116.

11 Werner Rodek, in: Limberg/Rübsaat, eds., *Nach dem "Anschluss,"* 94.

12 Adunka et al, eds., *Exilforschung: Österreich;* see also my essay "Exile Studies in Austria," in: Günter Bischof/David Wineroither, eds., *Democracy in Austria* (Contemporary Austrian Studies 28) (New Orleans-Innsbruck: UNO Press/Innsbruck University Press, 2019), 309-18.

PREFACE
JOSHUA PARKER

Eighty years later, we might romantically be tempted to think of them as exiles. But they were refugees.

They certainly saw themselves as such. Of the estimated four percent of Austrians targeted on political or racial grounds after Austria joined Hitler's Third Reich (the *Anschluss*) in 1938, some 135,000 fled the country, among them an estimated 1,200 writers. An almost equal number of Austrian authors who stayed behind did not survive. It's been claimed that "no land occupied by the fascists, not even the German Reich itself, could show a higher proportion of its writers forced into involuntary exile than Austria."[1] All in all, some 30,000 Europeans fled Austria to the United States just before and during the Second World War, to an America that still has yet to hear their voices or their stories in translation.

This volume brings together voices previously unavailable to English-speaking readers, from a world refugee crisis to which that of our own time can, as yet, only claim second standing. Voices who found a home, temporary or permanent, in America, when they might otherwise have been extinguished. Out of pride or shame, they often called themselves emigrés, *apatrides*, emigrants, immigrants or, in the politically-correct jargon of their own era,

---

1 Anthony Bushell, "Many Happy Returns? Attitudes to Exile in Austria's Literary and Cultural Journals in the early Post-war Years," in: *"Immortal Austria?" Austrians in Exile in Britain*. Ed. C. Brinson, R. Dove and J. Taylor (Amsterdam and New York: Rodopi, 2007), 198.

"newcomers." But they were refugees, asylum-seekers, migrants. "Driven from country to country," they represented, Hannah Arendt wrote, "the vanguard of their peoples—if they [kept] their identity." Yet, wrote Franz Carl Weiskopf, "There is no way to the inner vision than the outer one. The new country in which we live influences our choice of materials, influences the form. The outer landscape of the poet changes his inner."[2]

The authors collected here were, in every sense, a lost generation. Thankful, as Hermann Broch put it, "for a new page," whether already famous or still unknown, Austrian authors all became anonymous on reaching America. "And so all of a sudden the understanding, no, the horror, rose up in me," Georg Troller wrote, "that I didn't even have my own language anymore, me, the aspiring 'poet.' As if one had amputated a football player's leg."[3] "I'm not a bitter person," poet Mimi Grossberg said in later years of having to flee her home in 1938 to escape Auschwitz, which claimed the lives of her parents: "Just the opposite. What should I hate? I only hate one thing: that I was forced to live in a land with a foreign language."[4] With their books banned in German-speaking lands and the number of German-speaking Americans themselves having dropped dramatically after the First World War, they were often left feeling, as Max Roden did, like a shepherd without a flock. Even if careers and dreams of such displaced persons were not always, as Roden worried, "Blüten im Schnee" (blossoms in snow), their work often remained, Erich Fried wrote, a body of poetry with no homeland. For writers, "exile had been particularly painful. Whereas musicians, scientists, architects, painters and many other categories of

2 Franz Carl Weiskopf, "Sprache im Exil," in: Über Literatur und Sprach: Literarische Streifzüge Verteidigung der Deutschen Sprache (Berlin: Dietz Verlag, 1960), 483.
3 Georg Stefan Troller, *Wohin und zurück: Die Axel-Corti-Trilogie* (Vienna: Theodor Kramer Gesellschaft, 2009), 50.
4 Cited in Gerhard Jelinek, *Nachrichten aus dem 4. Reich* (Salzburg: Ecowin Verlag, 2008), 86.

intellectuals were free—in theory at least—to continue to practice their professions when once established in their new world, writers with few exceptions could not. Their lifeblood was the German language and it was only within a German-speaking world that they, with few exceptions, could ply their trade."[5] Stefan Zweig, in New York as his works were banned (and literally burned) in occupied countries, described feeling like an actor playing to an empty theater. But he remained, he wrote, a patriot of a foreign land.

Franz Theodor Csokor described the Viennese as Hitler arrived in April 1938 as elated as if a fairytale from *One Thousand and One Nights* had just begun.[6] By 1939, Europe seemed, from his exile, a sinking ship, forever having new holes drilled into its hull.[7] "I knew," wrote Mimi Grossberg of those years, "something was going on, that they would kill us all, I already knew that. But I didn't think of concentration camps with gas chambers. That was their idea. No normal person comes up with an idea like that."[8] As early as 1933, Günther Anders argued that all Jewish refugees from Europe, having been used by Hitler for political purposes, were "political refugees," by default.[9] By September 1939 there were already three separate organizations for Austrian refugees in New York (the Austrian-American League, the Austrian-American Society, and the Austrian-American Center), largely formed around political affiliation with now defunct parties from the homeland.[10] Settling most densely in and around Washington Heights, some 60,000 German-speaking

---

5 Bushell, "Many Happy Returns," 198.

6 Franz Theodor Csokor, *Auch heute noch nicht an Land: Briefe und Gedichte aus dem Exil*, ed. Franz Richard Reiter (Vienna: Ephelant Verlag, 1993), 176.

7 Ibid., 227.

8 Cited in Jelinek, *Nachrichten aus dem 4. Reich*, 82.

9 Anthony Heilbut, Anthony *Exiled in Paradise: German Refugee Artists and Intellectuals in America, from the 1930s to the Present* (New York: Viking, 1983), 24.

10 Franz Goldner, *Die Österreichische Emigration 1938 bis 1945* (Vienna: Verlag Harold, 1977), 86.

immigrants called their new home "the fourth Reich," or, more hopefully, "the second republic." By 1941, only forty-seven percent of Austrian visa applications to the United States were accepted, due to quotas. By 1942, only seventeen percent of applications were accepted.[11] In February 1942, Otto von Habsburg convinced the US government to no longer consider Austrian immigrants as enemy foreigners, which eased their situation.[12] But in the years following the war, as traumatized Europeans still fled for the United States, it is estimated the country rejected eighty to eighty-five percent of Austrian visa applications.[13] Max Reinhardt, founder of the Salzburg Festival, before dying in New York in 1943, complained that Americans, "daily bombarded with horrifying news," had numbed themselves to the refugees' plight, arming themselves "against everything that doesn't affect them personally. It's [...] like a gasmask, which one consciously or unconsciously puts on, then which isn't so easily removed," or like "the rich man in the fable who, hassled for help by an unfortunate man, calls his servants: Take this man away! He's breaking my heart!"[14]

They "worked by day and wrote by night," their "night-time language" allowing them a degree of continuity in their lives, until their workday hours, in factories, shops, or small businesses, seemed "no more than holes in the fabric of [their] live.."[15] "The refugee suffers homesickness for a country he can no longer call his home," wrote Troller. "He finds himself in an in-between kingdom."[16] This intermediate space was

---

11 Jelinek, *Nachrichten aus dem 4. Reich*, 21.

12 Goldner, *Die Österreichische Emigration*, 112.

13 Jelinek, *Nachrichten aus dem 4. Reich*, 21.

14 Max Reinhardt, "Resignation: 1943." In: *Max Reinhardt Schriften: Briefe, Aufsätze, Interviews, Gespräche, Auszüge aus Regiebüchern*, ed. H. Fetting (Berlin: Henschelverlag Kunst und Gesellschaft, 1974), 254.

15 Kerstin Putz, "Improvised Lives: Günther Anders's American Exile." *Quiet Invaders Revisited: Biographies of Twentieth Century Immigrants to the United States*, ed. Günter Bischof (Innsbruck: StudienVerlag, 2017), 240.

16 Troller, *Wohin und zurück*, 55.

often experienced as bearing refractions of both lands. Like the
"double vision" described by Walter Abish, Austrian authors in
America often could not help feeling they floated between two
distinct visions of their environment. For Lore Segal, arriving
in New York in 1951 after more than a decade in exile from her
hometown of Vienna as a child refugee, Times Square seemed
like an over-animated Viennese Christmas market.[17] "The
refugee has to shamefully rebuild things from the language of
his new environment into the old one! Language is more than a
'system of signs that serves a community for understanding.' It's
also a network of symbols, of associations, of meaning-images
based on shared experience," wrote Troller.[18] This network of
new memories associated with places, Segal imagined, is "the
way our histories become charged thus upon the air, the streets,
the very houses of New York, that makes the alien into a citizen,"
on an island of comforts "surrounded on all sides by calamity."[19]
Indeed, an "island of the blessed." Such a network was in active
formation during the 1930s, 1940s and 1950s as Austrian
writers found themselves both estranged from and comforted
by notions of two lands. Their poems evoke the state of being
stateless, a situation and status unfortunately all too common in
our own time.

"The streets are paved with gold, but I only find chewing gums,"
joked musician Fritz Spielmann.[20] Landing, for many for the
first time, in perhaps the world's most bustling, industrialized
metropolis, writers tempered their shock in words. Their
thoughts sought translation, and poetry was a comforting
medium: lines, verses and rhymes are at least some way to
make familiar the unfamiliar. Their thoughts as they walked
Manhattan's streets, if we can take any measure of them from

17 Lore Segal, *Other People's Houses* (New York: The New Press, 1990), 286.
18 Troller, *Wohin und zurück*, 55.
19 Segal, *Other People's Houses*, 311f.
20 Cited in Jelinek, *Nachrichten aus dem 4. Reich*, 170.

their verses, ran in repetitive, circular rhythms, not just the daily rhythm of New York's streets, parks, and harbors, but that of a death industry they half-knew ran in tandem, its motor engaged and running full-speed, back on the other side of the Atlantic.

Ernst Waldinger, an Austrian author resettled in New York, compared himself to an old-fashioned city horse in the bustling metropolis of automobiles: "—a horse stands mid the autos' muddle / With clumsy hooves and restless muzzle. / Did he not just nod at me as I did at him likewise? / Like me toward him he gazed with tired eyes, / As if the question stood dully in his mind: / Are you as lonely here as I?" Waldinger actively shepherded his and others' flocks of German-speaking readers, in 1944 helping found the Aurora publishing house in New York, winning the Vienna literature prize in 1960, and remaining in the United States until his death. Aurora gave a voice to authors writing in German whose audience had been closed to them in Europe, publishing, among others, Joseph Wechsberg, who, after fleeing the Gestapo to the United States, also wrote in English for *The New Yorker*, a magazine itself co-founded by Austrian Raoul Fleischmann, its president for over thirty-five years.[21] The Austrian Institute, now the Austrian Cultural Forum, was founded in New York in 1942. In this sense, and others, Austrians were ahead of Americans in working in the other's country as a cultural disseminator—as the United States would only be doing after the war with their own America Houses.

Psychotherapist and author Alfred Farau, another resident of Washington Heights's "Fourth Reich," suggested that in order to recover from the violence his postwar compatriots had experienced in expulsion and flight, each ought to return at least once to Austria, to cure the psychic pain of their memories.[22] But

---

21 E. Wilder Spaulding, *The Quiet Invaders: The Story of the Austrian Impact Upon America* (Vienna: Österreichischer Bundesverlag für Unterricht, Wissenschaft und Kunst, 1968), 158f.
22 Cited in Jelinek, *Nachrichten aus dem 4. Reich*, 84.

going back often proved as uncanny an experience as had first arriving in America. One of Segal's protagonists, recognizing her own former Viennese building, cries, "'Here it is! [...] You see! The corner door!'" Recognition of one's own former home "had that odd little importance one feels in presenting certification—a driver's license, a library card: this proves that this is me [...] It is I who lived here." Yet remembering, Segal suggested, "is a complicated act. The often-documented alteration of the size of the object, because of the viewer's altered size, is its simplest aspect." Then there was "that coincidence of the ghostly, transparent, unstable stuff memory is made of, with the hard-edged material object, which, as often as not, is, in fact, altered [...] And there is the degree of history the viewer shares with the view, whether it's the fact, merely, of having passed, or of having been at home here, where his neighbor had hated him to death."[23] Max Roden ironically published in the series "Neue Dichtung aus Österreich," though Roden himself had been living in New York by that point for nineteen years, writing of a 1958 visit to the city of his birth, Vienna: "Not house, not street do I want to see. / The door is closed. The window darkened. / I must go to the other Vienna, / which doesn't weary in darkness."[24] Viennese publisher Frederick Ungar, whose press was "Aryanized" in 1938 and who then fled to America, asked years later if he still considered Austria his home, replied, "I think my mother tongue is the true home. [...] Language is homeland for me."[25]

It was perhaps Grossberg who worked hardest over her lifetime to collect and preserve the voices of this lost generation. Kurt Hampe, head of the Austrian Information Service in New York from 1959-1967, in the introduction to Grossberg's poetry anthology *Kleinkunst aus Amerika*, admitted that, over the years

23 Segal, *Other People's Houses*, 264.
24 Max Roden, "In Wien 1958," in: *Tod und Mond und Glas* (Vienna: Bergland Verlag, 1959), 50.
25 Cited in Jelinek, *Nachrichten aus dem 4. Reich*, 194.

of his work in America, nothing had touched him so deeply as "the ring of those voices which, though far from home, preserve their language," comparing his encounter with these poets to that of a hiker who, "on foreign and sometimes hard, rough ground, suddenly comes across flowers he imagined could only be grown in a domestic garden back home," wafting "with bittersweet scents of homesickness and memory, but also of a bracing American strength." Such writing has long sat in a sort of national limbo. It is American. And it is Austrian. Yet it remains foreign to both.

In postwar Austria, exile would not, Miguel Herz-Kestranek, Konstantin Kaiser and Daniela Stringl write, come to be seen as a part of Austrian history and identity, so that, even today, two parallel literatures exist in Austria, unreconciled, without overlapping—that of the exiles often ignored or treated as slightly alien. Meanwhile, though a large proportion of Austrian refugee authors in the United States remained there permanently after the war, their words and very existence has been easily overlooked by American readers. This volume hopes to compensate a little. It has two goals, one direct, the other more implicit: to claim a body of poetry, as much as it may be Austrian, as also properly American; and to reflect on the crises of more contemporary refugees, reminding us that, eighty years ago, many Americans considered people and authors we would today think of as "white Europeans" fleeing war and genocide to be undesirable, even dangerous, alien invaders from an enemy state and of a minority race and religion.

The volume includes two lyric prose texts by Stefan Zweig and Franz Carl Weiskopf expressing the bewilderment of Europeans facing modern New York for the first time, and the comfort generations of exiles and refugees found in cultural loci of Manhattan catering to literature they found familiar. It also includes authors, like Theodor Kramer who, though escaping the Holocaust in England, spent a lifetime promoting refugee and resistance literature through contacts with writers in the United States, and Erich Fried, who also sought refuge in England, but whose active engagement with US politics, and work as a translator of US authors, put him in the company of American intellectuals and writers of the second half of the twentieth century. Indeed, Fried's residence in England seems to have allowed him a more objective (and critical) view of US postwar foreign actions than that afforded to many of his peers in the United States.

Poetry is one of the simplest ways of registering political dissent and resistance, but also of showcasing irony and wit. These works highlight such dissent as it found voice in its own native language, for an audience neither wide nor obvious at the time, but which still speaks to us today. These voices from the refugee crisis of the mid-twentieth century, as a narrative, present a hopeful story whose themes resonate in our own present even more clearly, and perhaps with even more pressing pertinence. Some of the best voices of their day, they speak with timely comments on the American experience and on America itself.

Salzburg, 2019

Blossoms in Snow:

Austrian Refugee Poets in Manhattan

JULIUS BUCHWALD, born in Vienna in 1909, was a world chess champion, composer, painter, and stamp collector. He left Austria for England after the 1938 *Anschluss*, and was interned on the Isle of Man. Through the efforts of his sister, Mimi Grossberg, he secured a US visa, reaching New York in 1946, and living in Queens until his death in 1970.

Ich reise durch die Welt

aus *Emigrantenlieder*

Ich reise durch die Welt,
durch Städte, Dörfer, Wald und Feld.
Per Auto, Flugzeug, Bahn, zu Fuss;
ich atme Dampf, Benzin und Russ.
Die Brise braust mir ins Gesicht,
steh ich auf Deck im Sternenlicht.
Fabriken qualmen mir vorbei
und Hämmer dröhnen Erz zu Brei.
Chinesen lächeln scheu, verschmitzt,
des Negers Zahnreih blendend blitzt.

Und ich, ich reise durch die Welt;
durch Städte, Dörfer, Wald und Feld.
Per Auto, Flugzeug, Bahn, zu Fuss;
beneid mich nicht darum – ich muss!

I Travel Through the World
from *Emigrant Songs*

I travel through the world,
through cities, towns, forest, field.
By car, airplane, train, on foot;
I breathe steam, gasoline and soot.
The breeze rushes in my face,
as I stand in starlight on the deck.
Factories puff past me
as hammers pound ore to paste.
Asians smile shyly, mischievous,
the African's sparkling teeth flash.

And I, I travel through the world;
through cities, towns, forest, field.
On foot, by car, by train or bus;
Don't envy me for that – I must!

Begegnung
aus *Emigrantenlieder*

Wir leben hier und dort auf der Welt,
So wie es dem lieben Schicksal gefällt.
Wir ziehen uns an wie die Sterne,
Seh'n wir uns an,
Und wissen schon dann:
„Das muss doch einer von uns sein!"

Wir möchten ihn fragen,
Ohn es zu wagen:
„Woher kommst du? Wie heisst du?
Was hast du mitgemacht?
Wen kennst du? Was tu'st du?
Wozu hast d's gebracht?"

Doch gehen wir unserer Wege,
Als ob uns nicht daran läge.
Wir verlieren uns dann in der Ferne,
Weit weg, sowie kreisende Sterne.

Encounter

from *Emigrant Songs*

We live here and there on this earth,
Scattered by destiny, birth.
Attracting each other like stars,
Only needing look at each other
To know:
"That must be one of our own!"

We want to ask,
Without daring:
"Where are you from? What's your name?
What have you been through?
Who do you know? What do you do?
What have you been up to?"

But each turns his own way,
As if nought were in play.
Losing ourselves in the far,
Drawn distant, like circling stars.

FREDERICK (FRITZ) BRAININ, born in Vienna in 1913, studied philosophy, was a member of the "Rote Falken," and was in contact with the literary "Gruppe der Jungen" and "Das politische Kabarett." He wrote short theater pieces, publishing his poetry and prose in newspapers, and in 1934 became the Vienna correspondent for US-based Seven Arts Feature Syndicate. In 1938 he fled through Italy to New York, where he published poetry in journals and anthologies. From 1942-1945 he served in the US army. Captured as a prisoner of war, he suffered serious psychological trauma, afterward finding himself only able to write and speak in English. At around the age of 70, he began to recover his use of German, making increasing contacts in Vienna, and eventually writing radio plays for Austrian radio. He died in New York in 1992.

Nuovo York

Sohn eines Bildhauers,
geboren am linken Ufer Wiens,
schrieb ich auf (auf Deutsch!)
Verse, Tagebücher,
die ich überlebte.
Schon bald traf Hermann Göring
auf seinem Pegasus ein.

Der "Tag", inzwischen ein Naziblatt,
brachte irrtümlich Verse von mir . . .
Ich packte meine Sachen:
Die reine Flamme meiner Gedichte stand auf dem Spiel.

Im Juni '38
las ich nachts bei einer geheimen Zusammenkunft Lieder
(wir blieben lang auf für die Kurzwellenübertagung des Kampfes Louis –
Schmeling!).
Ich reiste ab, nach Venedig
(narrte die schwarze Flughafen-SS mit meinem Tennisschläger!)
um dem Erdball meine Liebe zu erklären:

Neun Priester und ich taten uns zusammen, zu einem Minjan;
der Windhund gehörte einer Hure,
die am Lido ihren Geschäften nachging,
ich hingegen ging dorthin, meinen Stil zu kurieren.

Zwischen Algier und Lissabon
brachte mich die Salzgischt der S.S. Vulcania zum Weinen . . .
Wir hielten vor den grünen Azoren,
wo mit Zeiss-Kameras bewaffnete Gaffer
den Sprung eines Luftmenschen (mitten zwischen Delphine!)
schnappschossen.

Nuovo York

Son of a sculptor,
born on Vienna's left bank,
I penned (in German!)
verses, diaries,
which I survived.
Soon enough Hermann Goering
arrived on his Pegasus.

The *Tag*, meanwhile, a Nazi newspaper,
printed my verses by mistake . . .
I packed my things:
The pure flame of my poems was at stake.

In June '38
I read songs at a secret night reunion
(we stayed up late for the shortwave transfer of the fight of Louis —
Schmeling!).[1]
I left for Venice
(fooled the black airport-SS with my tennis racquet!)
to declare my love to the planet:

Nine priests and I met together, in a Minyan;
the greyhound belonged to a whore,
who pursued her business at the Lido,
I, however, went there to cure my style.

Between Algiers and Lisbon
the salt spray of the S.S. Vulcania brought me to tears . . .
We stopped before the green Azores,
where gapers armed with Zeiss cameras
captured the jump of a man (between dolphins!)
in snapshots.[2]

---

1   A Yankee Stadium boxing match between German Max Schmeling and Alabama-born African-American Joe Louis. Schmeling, having beat Louis two years earlier, to the Nazi regime's open praise, lost the match in June 1938. The face-off, with 70,000 in attendance, drew international attention as a live, real-time allegory for contemporary racialist theories. Harlem's streets filled with tens of thousands of celebrators at the end of the match. "With their faces to the night sky," reported Richard Wright that summer, "they filled their lungs with air and let out a scream of joy that it seemed would never end, a scream that seemed to come from untold reserves of strength."

2   The poem was likely originally written in English, then translated to German by Hans Raimund. It is unclear if the original English was ever published.

ALBERT EHRENSTEIN was born in Vienna in 1886, where he completed a doctorate in history in 1910. A friend of psychologist Alfred Adler, a member of the first Dadaist magazine, and co-founder of a still-successful press, he published short stories, essays, and expressionist poetry illustrated by Oskar Kokoschka. Traveling through the Middle East in the 1920s, he became critical of the colonial powers' "bomb culture." His books were burned in Germany in 1933. In Switzerland, where he would spend the next nine years, forbidden to publish by the Swiss authorities, he founded a committee to help refugees from the German Reich. He arrived in New York in 1941, where he wrote for newspapers, dying nine years later in a pauper's hospice.

Emigrantenlied
(gekürzt)

Das war der Frieden: du hattest Ruh,
Arbeit hienieden – im Himmel stempelst du.
Dann sind die braunen Wuthunde gekommen
Und haben ein Reich, ein zweites, ein drittes genommen.
Kein Kampf – man hat sich dumpf ergeben,
Schöner als Zwangsrobot schien: Im Frieden leben.
Aber der Freiheit Licht
findest du nicht,
Man hat längst in elender Länder Gossen
Sie unverdrossen auf der Flucht erschossen.
....
Wer seine Heimat unterwegs im Strassenraub verloren,
Wer sein lieb Vaterland durch Naziraub verloren –
Kein Passpapier? Zurück mit dir!
Visum ins Nichts! Hier bist du nicht geboren!

Emigrant Song
(excerpt)[1]

That was freedom: you had quiet,
Work down here — welfare in heaven.
Then came the brown mad dogs
And took a Reich, a second, a third.
No fight — one surrendered dully,
Better than forced labor seemed: Living in peace.
But you don't find
freedom's light,
Since they shot freedom on the run
Long ago, tirelessly in wretched countries' gutters.
. . . .

Those who lost their homeland to street robbery on the way,
Those who lost their beloved country through Nazi theft —
No passport? Back with you!
A visa to nowhere! You weren't born here![2]

---

1 Evidently shortened by Mimi Grossberg in 1985.
2 "Passport to Nowhere" is the title of a 1938 short story by Budd Schulberg,
about a Jewish Polish painter pushed out of his home by a pogrom and trying
to reach Palestine.

BERTHOLD VIERTEL, born in Vienna in 1885, studied philosophy, then worked as a theater director in Vienna, Dresden, Berlin, and Düsseldorf, publishing his first volume of poetry in 1913 and beginning to direct films in 1922. After working in New York and California, he returned to Berlin in 1932, leaving his family behind in Hollywood. As Hitler rose to power, he fled to Vienna, then to London, where he co-founded the *German Anti-Nazi Monthly*, before returning to New York in 1939. He published articles on the political situation in Europe during the war, edited two volumes of poetry, and translated work by Tennessee Williams. His writings include theater pieces and some 2000 poems. He returned to Vienna in 1948 and was a director at the Burgtheater, dying in Vienna in 1953.

Auswanderer

Nun müssen wir von allem scheiden,
Was Kindheit uns und Wachstum war.
Wir sollen selbst die Sprache meiden,
Die unserer Herzen Wort gebar.

Die Landschaft werden wir verlassen,
Die uns auf ihren Armen trug.
Wir sollen diese Wälder hassen
Und hatten ihrer nie genug.

Wie je uns wieder anvertrauen
Dem Friedenshauche einer Flur,
Wenn Abendlicht und Morgengrauen
Befleckt sind mit der blutigen Spur?

Wenn in der Bäume gutem Raunen
Aufrauscht der Hass, der uns vertreibt!
Es lernten unsre Kinder staunen,
Warum man nicht zu Hause bleibt?

Wir sind, mein Kind, nie mehr zuhause,
Vergiss das Wort, vergiss das Land
Und mach im Herzen eine Pause –
Dann gehn wir. Wohin? Unbekannt.

Emigrants

Now we must divorce from all
That was childhood and youth.
We must even avoid the language,
Which bore our hearts' word.

We will leave the landscape,
Which carried us in its arms.
We should hate these forests
And could never get enough of them.

How shall we ever again trust
In a meadow's peaceful breezes,
When evening's light and morning's gray
Are flecked with bloody traces?

If in the trees' good murmurs
The hate that expels us rustles!
Our children ask, amazed,
Why don't we stay at home?

We're never at home again, my child,
Forget the land, forget the word
And let your heart settle a short while —
Then we'll go. Where? Unknown.

Gekritzel auf der Rückseite eines Reisepasses

Man ward mit keinem Paß geboren.
Die Sprache lernte man als Kind.
Am Ende ging der Sinn verloren
Der Worte, die gebräuchlich sind.

Was Heimat heißt, nun heißt es Hölle,
Der man zur rechten Zeit entkam.
Und neue Grenzen, neue Zölle,
Doch selten wo ein wenig Scham.

Das sind die Orte und die Zeiten.
Einst war man jung, nun wird man alt.
Doch immerzu muß man bestreiten
Die Reise und den Aufenthalt.

Das sind die Völker und die Reiche.
Man wandert aus und wandert ein.
Doch überall ist das Gleiche:
Die Hirne Wachs, die Herzen Stein.

Doodle on the Back of a Passport

One isn't born with a passport.
Language is learned as a child.
In the end, the meaning was lost
Of the words which are most worthwhile.

What's called homeland is now called hell,
which you escaped just in time.
And new borders, new checkpoints,
But rarely anywhere much shame.

Those are the places and the times.
First you were young, now you grow older.
But you must always tackle
The journey and the layover.

Those are the peoples and empires.
Out and in you roam.
But everywhere it's the same:
Minds of wax, hearts of stone.

Ohne Decke, ohne Kohlen

Ohne Decke, ohne Kohlen,
Frierend bis in die Gedärme,
Züge, vollgepfercht, nach Polen:
Juden brauchen keine Wärme.

Eine dichte Unglückswolke,
Abgetriebene Menschheitsbeute.
Nicht von Völkern, sprecht vom Volke:
Sagt nicht Juden, heißt die Leute!
Nicht verfilzten Kornes Garben,
Die ein Wucherer verschoben,
Sondern Sterbende, die darben,
Bald der Lebenslast enthoben.

Einer Fremde zugetrieben,
Bis sie wo im Dreck verenden,
Und sie konnten ihren Lieben
Nicht ein Sterbenswörtchen senden.

Alte Männer, alte Frauen,
In ein Land, sie nicht zu nähren,
Wo sie keine Häuser bauen,
Sie, die niemals wiederkehren.

Zöllnersohn, er hat's befohlen,
Sohn der Magd, sein Herz zu heilen:
Ohne Decken, ohne Kohlen
In den Tod, endlose Meilen.

Without Blanket, without Coals

Without blanket, without coals,
Freezing down to your bones,
Trains, packed full for Poland:
Jews require no warmth.

A thick cloud of bad luck,
Driven out, human loot.
Don't speak of peoples, speak of people:
Don't say Jews, they're people!
Not matted sheaves of grain,
Moved by a profiteer,
But the dying, who starve,
Soon relieved of life's burden.

Driven into a foreign land,
To die in the dirt somewhere,
Unable to send their loved-ones
A single dying word.

Old men, old women,
Into a land that won't feed them,
Where they'll build no houses,
They, who never return.

The son of a customs officer, son of the maid,[1]
To heal his heart, has ordered them:
Without blankets, without coals
To their deaths, endless miles.

---

1 Adolf Hitler was raised by a customs official and a housekeeper in Upper
Austria.

ULRICH BECHER was born in Berlin in 1910. A life-long friend of George Grosz, he was a regular fixture of the Weimar Republic's literary and artistic scene. His first play's opening premier at the Berlin Volksbühne was banned when Nazis took power in 1933, and he was the youngest author to have a book burned by Nazis. He moved to Austria, taking Austrian citizenship, and married the daughter of Roda Roda. In 1938 he took the last train out of Austria for Switzerland. When France fell to Hitler, he fled to Rio de Janeiro, writing for antifascist newspapers. He moved to New York in 1944 to care for his father-in-law, who died the very day the war ended. His four years in New York were spent in poverty, but in the company of Grosz, and of figures like John Dos Passos, Edmund Wilson, Henry Miller, and Sinclair Lewis. Returning to Vienna in 1948 before moving back to Switzerland, he died in 1990. He was co-editor of the "Notbücherei deutscher Antifaschisten" and wrote novels, short stories, theater pieces, and novellas, including *New Yorker Novellen* (1969).

Der schwarze Segler

Wir zogen aus ins Meer.
In Schiffes Bauch das Echo klang
von schwerem Tritt. Kein Vogel sang,
zu lindern die Beschwer.

Wir rauschen ein ins Nichts.
Das Segel schwellt, ein schwarzes Tuch;
wir kehren uns dem Grossen Fluch,
Entlassne des Gerichts.

Wir ziehn in giftge Fern.
Bis grünes Finster uns umquoll
und uns ein letzter Gruss verscholl:
der Kindheit erster Stern.
Flugfischen zugesellt.
Die Schwinge schwarz im weissen Wind
entführt uns meerschaumhaft Gesind,
wohin es ihr gefällt.

Delphinenpurzelbaum!
Die dicke Wolk am Himmelsrand
gleich einem Riesenelefant
in Schlaf gestreckt und Traum…

Nach einem Mond zur Nacht
tost aus dem Meer ein Ruf empor,
Drommeten-Pauken-Pfeifenchor,
davon wir all erwacht.

Der Sturm spie uns an Strand.
Kaum retteten wir Hose, Hemd.
Ein dunkles Antlitz schaut uns fremd.
Wir haben's nicht erkannt.

The Black Sailboat

We set out to sea.
In the ship's belly the echo rang
from a heavy step. No bird sang,
to soften the decree.

We rush into the blankness of sea.
The sail swells, a black sheet;
we turn away from the great curse,
Expelled by legal decree.

We pull into the poisonous far.
Till green darkness overcame us
and a last greeting was lost to us:
childhood's first star.
Our companions are flying fishes.
The boom black in the white wind,
draws us, seafoam-filled serfs,
where it wishes.

Dolphin somersault!
The thick cloud where the sky bent
like a monstrous elephant
stretched in sleep and dreams . . .

After a moon through the night
a call cries from the sea's mire,
Trumpet-tympanum-pipe choir,
at which we all rose upright.

The storm spit us up on the beach.
Hardly had we rescued shirt, pants.
A dark face looked at us, askance.
We didn't recognize its speech.

Mann furchtlos hingesehn.
Trockne dein Hemd und fürcht dich nicht;
Es ist des Menschen Angesicht.
Du darfst, du darfst bestehn.

Man with no help left for you.
Dry your shirt, put fear away;
It is a human face.
You may, you may come through.

SANEL BEER was born in 1886 in Vienna, where he worked as a doctor before fleeing via Italy to the United States in 1938. He was founder and president of the Austro-American Association (1953-1976) and the director of the Rivermont Park Sanatorium in Miami. It was during his exile that he began writing, publishing two volumes of poetry and a novel. He died in Miami in 1981.

Versagte Rettung

Es lächelt das Meer, die Möwe schwirrt
die Lüfte empor und hinab und girrt
im Haschen der Fische. Leicht bewegt
die See an die Küste schlägt
und wirft die Muscheln und Tang aus
in rhythmisch auf- und abschwellendem Braus.
Am Rande des Himmels in der Fern
ein Boot zieht sachte hin. Ein fahler Stern
im Dämmerlicht des Tages flimmert,
die Mondsichel durch die Wolken schimmert.
Um mich ist still die ganze Welt.
In ihrem Bann die Ruh mich hält.
Nur pochen höre ich mein Herz,
das immer wieder sich krümmt im Schmerz,
sich sehnend nach der geliebten Hand,
die an der anderen Küste Land
nach Hilfe ruft, die wir versagen.
Ihr Herz bricht nieder im Verzagen.

Denied Rescue

The sea smiles, the gull glides
on air, cooing, falls and rises
at the hooking of fish. Lightly troubled,
the sea beats on the coast
and throws the mussels and seaweed out
in rhythmic to- and fro-swelling waves.
At the sky's edge in the distance
a boat goes gently by. A pallid star
flickers in the day's twilight,
the crescent moon shines through the clouds.
Around me the whole world is still.
Its silence holds me in its spell.
Only throbbing hear I in my heart,
which constantly, painfully smarts,
yearning for the beloved hand,
which from the other coast of land
calls for help—we're unrespondent.
Her heart breaks down, despondent.

EGON FREY, born in Vienna in 1892, was a professor of medicine at the University of Vienna. Throughout the 1920s, he published magazine articles, short stories, novellas and a novel. He fled to New York in 1940, where he worked as a doctor and psychotherapist, dying in 1972.

Wenn Dunkel droht . . .

Die kleinen Lerchen sind schon aufgeflogen
Nach Süden hin, ans Meer.
Der Himmel, feindlich aller Wiederkehr,
Wälzt grau die Wolkenwogen.

Hat erst die See das Lerchenlied verschlungen,[1]
Ist aller Wohllaut tot.
Wo fliegt die Seele hin, wenn Dunkel droht?
Zu euch, Erinnerungen.

Ins Land, dem auch die Sonne stärker strahlt
Mit Strahlen, die im Winter nicht ermüden.
Vergangenheit, vom Sehnen hellgemalt,
Sei armer Seelen Süden! –

---

1 *Lerchenlied*, Bernart de Ventador (1135-1194).

When Darkness Threatens . . .

The little larks have flown away
To the South, to the sea.
The sky, hostile of all return,
Rolls the cloud-waves gray.

Once the sea has swallowed the lark's song,
All euphony is dead.
Where does the soul fly when darkness threatens?
To you, memories.

To the country where the sun shines stronger
With rays in winter untiring.
Past, painted bright by longing,
Be the poor man's South! —

GUIDO ZERNATTO, born in 1903 in Carinthia, published essays and novels, winning a German literature prize for a collection of short stories in 1930. In 1934 he began working as a state secretary for the Austrian chancellor's office. In 1938, as the SS marched into his office building, he fled to Czechoslovakia, making his way through Hungary and Italy to France with a fake French passport (awkwardly unable to speak French to the customs control on arriving at the border). He hoped to set up an Austrian government in exile in Paris, but fled to Portugal in 1940 when France was invaded. When the Third Reich sent an order for his extradition from Portugal, unable to secure a US visa, he entered New York as a tourist, reapplied, and, after crossing the Canadian border, reentered the United States with an immigrant visa. He taught at Fordham University before dying of heart disease in 1943.

Aus tausend Quellen quillt die Nacht

Aus tausend Quellen quillt die Nacht
Und übernimmt den Himmel unsrer Träume.
Da ist nichts mehr. Sintflut. Nur noch Nacht.

Aus Ozeanen ohne Licht erheben sich Gedanken,
Wie Meerestiere schwimmen unsre Träume
Mit schweren Flossen durch die Finsternis der Räume
Und kreisen um die Hoffnungsschiffe, die versanken.

The Night Swells from a Thousand Springs

The night swells from a thousand springs
And takes over the sky of our dreams.
Nothing's left. Flood. Only night.

From lightless oceans our thoughts rise,
Like sea creatures, our dreams swim
Through the darkness of space, with thick fins
Circling hope-ships, which capsized.

New York, 1942

Dieser Wind der fremden Kontinente

Dieser Wind der fremden Kontinente
Bläst mir noch die Seele aus dem Leib.
Nicht das Eis lähmt mir das frostgewohnte
Und die Schwüle nicht das langentthronte
Herz, das leer ist wie ein ausgeweintes Weib.

Dieser Wind der fremden Kontinente
Hat den Atem einer andern Zeit.
Andre Menschen, einer andern Welt geboren,
Mag's erfrischen. Ich bin hier verloren
Wie ein Waldtier, das in Winternächten schreit.

This Wind of Foreign Continents

This wind of foreign continents
Blows the soul from my body.
My heart, used to frost, isn't paralyzed by cold
Nor by humidity, long-dethroned
Heart, empty as a woman all cried out.

This wind of foreign continents
Has the breath of another time.
Other people, in another world born,
may find it refreshing. I'm forlorn
Like a forest animal, crying in winter nights.[1]

New York, 1943

---

1 Zernatto died only a few days after writing this poem.

PAUL ELBOGEN was born in Vienna in 1894, and studied law and art history. From 1929-1935 he edited entertainment magazines in Berlin, while publishing novels under a pseudonym. In 1941 he fled through Italy, France (where he was interned), Spain and Portugal, finally reaching New York with the aid of the Emergency Rescue Committee and help from a brother who had escaped Dachau. With the support of Billy Wilder, he worked as a film consultant for Columbia Pictures, and supported himself by trading fruit juice, writing newspaper articles and lecturing on art history. He was killed in a car accident in 1987.

Ankunft

Wir ankern endlich in dem Hafenarm,
schon sieht man Häuserturm und Autobus.
Die Freiheitsstatue hebt zum Gruß den Arm.
Zum erstenmal ist es kein Hitlergruß.

Zum erstenmal wirst du hier atmen dürfen –
ein freier Bürger unter freien Bürgern,
seit sieben Jahren wieder Leben schlürfen,
entflohn durch echte Wunder den Erwürgern.

Hier steht die helle Welt dir wieder offen,
du magst nun rennen oder schlendern wollen.
Dir ist erlaubt nun, wiederum zu hoffen.
Wie lange war dir dies Gefühl verschollen!

Hier rast das Leben wie ein Steppenbrand,
granithart mußt du sein und feuerfest;
dies ist wahrhaftig kein Schlaraffenland,
in dem man dir zu Tränen Muße läßt.

Hab keine Angst – dir wird dies Leben leicht!
Hast du den Tod nicht eben überwältigt?
Für dich, Geprüften, der damit vergleicht,
ist dies nur neues Glück, vertausendfältigt!

Arrival

We anchor at last in the harbor's swarm,
already in sight are housetops, bus route.
The Statue of Liberty raises its arm.
For the first time in a while, it's no Nazi salute.

For the first time you will be allowed to breathe here —
a free citizen among free citizens,
sipping life again after seven years,
your stranglers escaped by real miracles.

Here to you the bright world stands open anew,
you may want to run or stroll.
You are now allowed to hope too.
How long since you last had this feeling, so whole!

Here life races like a steppe fire,
granite-hard must you be, and fireproof;
this is truly no land of milk and honey,
in which you're allowed time for tears.

Have no fear — this life will be easy for you!
Did you not just beat death's hold?
Compared with that, for you,
this is just new happiness, thousandfold!

MIMI GROSSBERG was born in Vienna in 1905, where she studied English literature and psychology, then worked as a librarian. She published her first volume of poetry in 1935, fleeing Austria when Hitler invaded in 1938, and arriving in Manhattan with five dollars. From New York, she attempted, but failed, to secure exit visas for her parents, both of whom died in Auschwitz. A volunteer air raid warden during the war, she worked as a copyist and piece worker in a small hat factory. Frequently laid off between seasons, she found time to write and to champion the work of Austrian refugee poets in the United States, publishing several collections of her own and others' poetry, and giving public lectures on Austrian authors. She died in New York in 1999. In 2012, Mimi-Grossberg-Gasse was named for her in Vienna.

Der amerikanische Zoll

Durch halb Europa gelangte ich glatt
ohne jeglichen Zolleclat.
„Ne rien á déclarer?" „Merci!"
„Nichts zu verzollen?" „Entschuldigen Sie!"
„Niente per delarare?" „Niente!"
„Grazia, Signora, cordialmente!"

Aber der amerikanische Zoll
arbeitet nicht in Moll!
Der Herr Beamte hat Zeit –
sehr viel Zeit –
und ist wirklich gescheit!
Wie kann man nur so gescheit sein?

An was für Dinge er denkt!
In die Koffer sieht er kaum,
das bleibt mir geschenkt.
Aber dann!
Warum ich zwei Handtaschen trage?
Ob ich vielleicht wage . . . ?
„Aber bitte, das sind meine Fotos!"
„Fotos?" sagt er –
„Die möchte ich sehen!
Sind sie kopiert?"
Ich bin schwer begeistert,
ganz echauffiert.
„Sie wollen sie sehen? Wirklich?"
Was für ein Glück!
Wird er sie durchgehen?
Stück für Stück?
Ich möchte sie ihm gern alle zeigen –
aber –

American Customs Control

Across half of Europe, I passed with full ease
 entirely untroubled by border police.
"Ne rien á déclarer?" "Merci!"
"Nichts zu verzollen?" "Entschuldigen Sie!"
"Niente per delarare?" "Niente!"
"Grazia, Signora, cordialmente!"

But American customs control
works so seriously toward its goal!
Its officer has time —
lots of time —
and an intelligence truly sublime!
How can one be so bright?

He thinks of everything!
In the suitcases hardly a glance,
which was a quite a blessing.
But then!
Why have I got two handbags there?
"Might one possibly dare . . . ?"
"But please, that's my photos!"
"Photos?" says he—
"Then I'll need to see!
Are they copied?"
I'm completely thrilled,
all aglow, eyes wide.
"You want to look through them? Really?"
What fun!
Would he go through them?
One by one?
I'd have been happy to give him full range —
but —

der Mann ist so eigen –
gleich hat er genug!
Ist er enttäuscht?
Was hat er vermutet? Betrug?

Jetzt aber hat er mich!
Mit einem Piff,
mit festem Griff
entreißt er der Tasche den Fund.
Was denkt er sich?
Was sucht er denn eigentlich?
Ach, dies Paketchen!
Wer weiß, was das ist?
Ein Stückchen Toast!
Wie schnell man vergißt!
Ich hatt' es beim Frühstück mir eingesteckt,
mich für den Vormittag eingedeckt.
Die Landung kann dauern, der Hunger wird groß . . .
Ich plante im voraus – ich dachte bloß –
„Sie sind doch ganz sicher die erste Person,
die Toast in die U.S. mitbringt! Pardon!"
Und, eh ich begreife, was ihn so erbost,
zerbröselt er wütend das Stückchen Toast.
Er macht ein enttäuschtes Gesicht – wirklich schade –
wie ungezuckerte Limonade.
Anscheinend findet er nicht, was er sucht,
doch irgendwas an mir erscheint ihm verrucht.
Ich hab ihn enttäuscht, das ist wirklich fatal.
Zum Glück beginnt er nicht noch einmal!
Nein, nein, jetzt entläßt er mich, o Ironie,
ganz ohne jegliche Zeremonie.
Ich aber ward seither von Zweifeln geplagt.
Wonach hat der Mann so fanatisch gejagt?
War es nach Diamanten? Nach Pornografien?

the man is so strange —
he's soon had enough!
Shuts the album, a slam!
What had he imagined? Some kind of scam?

But now he has me!
A sigh he lets slip,
as with a firm grip
he pulls from the bag his find.
What does he see?
What's he looking for, really?
Oh, this little package!
Now, what can that be?
A piece of toast!
How things slip from memory!
I'd packed it, with breakfast, wrapped up in my sack,
saving it, just in case, for a late morning snack.
Landings will be delayed, hunger's often one's lot . . .
So I'd saved it for later—with hardly a thought—
"You're certainly the very first person,
to bring toast with them to the U.S.! Beg your pardon!"
And before I can judge what had angered his head,
he furiously crumbles the wee bit of bread.
His gaze throws me shade
like sour lemonade.
Apparently he hasn't found what he sought
but something in me still seems not as it ought.
I've disappointed him, and that's a real sin.
Lucky me that he doesn't start over again.
No, no, now he lets me pass, oh irony,
completely without further ceremony.
But doubts plagued me afterward, leaving me curious.
For what had the man been hunting, so furious?
Was it for diamonds? For pornography?

Oder – litt er an einem besonderen Spleen?
Ich zerbrach mir den Kopf – mittags, abends und früh.
Ach, solch eine Sache erklärt sich wohl nie . . .

Erst als ich das Rätsel beiseite schob,
bedauernd, verärgert, ja beinahe grob –
durchfuhr es mich plötzlich! Natürlich!
(greift sich an die Stirn)   DOPE!

Or — was he plagued by eccentricity?
Noon, morning and nights I kept wracking my brain.
Ach, such a thing's sometimes never explained . . .

Just as I'd let this strange riddle elope,
apologetically, angrily, a vulgar trope —
it hit me suddenly! But of course!
(gripping forehead)   DOPE![1]

    1938

---

1 In English, with explanatory note, in the original.

The Listener
(original English)

Sometimes, I stop at strangers' doors,
held back by secret strings.
I cannot move, my ears are caught:
The radiator sings.

Inside, the heat is hissing up,
inside, good spirits roam,
inside, the radiator sings,
inside, there is a home.

Outside, there is: a stranger's door,
a chilly winter night,
outside, there is nostalgia,
uncertainty, and fright.

That's why my heart begins to thaw,
my soul grows secret wings,
whenever through a stranger's door
a radiator sings.

Intermezzo in der New Yorker Untergrundbahn

Ein weisser Falter schwirrt verwirrt
durch einen Subwaywagen.
Der sah schon manchen selt'nen Gast
von rosa, gelber, grüner, brauner,
schwarzer Farbe.
Doch keiner konnte fliegen.
Dieser ist der erste seiner Art.
Wie kam er bloss herein?
Ward er von eines Fahrgasts
Blumenstrauss verlockt?
Oder vom hellen Imprimé
der Dame vis-à-vis?
Es folgen aller Augen wie gebannt
dem Flatterer,
der ratlos, rastlos, endlos, unermüdlich –
aus diesem Käfig einen Ausweg sucht.
Ist es sein Todestanz?
Mein Herz beginnt bereits mit ihm zu flattern . . .

Da – oh, ein Wunder:
Plötzlich dringt Tageslicht
von allen Seiten in den düstern Wagen.
"Onehundredtwentyfifth Street"
ruft der Schaffner,
die Türen öffnen sich,
fort ist der Flatterer.

Und alles nickt erlöst
einander zu.

Intermezzo in the New York Subway

A white butterfly whirrs, confused,
through a subway car.
Which saw many a rare passenger
of pink, yellow, green, brown,
black tones.
But none could fly.
This one is the first of its kind.
How did it ever get in?
Was it enticed
by a passenger's bouquet?
Or by the bright dress print
of the woman sitting across?
All eyes follow as if spellbound
the flutterer,
that helplessly, restlessly, endlessly, tirelessly—
from this cage seeks an exit.
Is this its death dance?
My heart already begins to flutter with him . . .

There—oh, a miracle:
Suddenly daylight penetrates
the gloomy car from every side.
"One Hundred Twenty-fifth Street"
calls the conductor,
the doors open,
the flutterer is gone.

And the passengers nod to each other
relieved.[1]

---

1 Grossberg's poem may be inspired by the previous generation of New York
Yiddish "Subway poets," who also focused in intimate vignettes taken from
the city's subway cars (Harshav).

STEFAN ZWEIG, born in Vienna in 1881, published his first short story collection in 1901 while still a student, then travelled widely after graduating. During the First World War, he worked in the Austrian war archives, until he could, as a pacifist and conscientious objector, make his way to Zürich. A world-famous, best-selling author during the 1920s and 1930s, he left Salzburg for London in 1935 as anti-Semitism in Austria became more and more disturbing, then moved to the United States in 1940. He died in Petropolis, Brazil, in 1942.

Hymnus an die Reise

Schienen, die blauen Adern aus Eisen,
Durchrinnen die Welt, ein rauschendes Netz.
Herz, rinn mit ihnen! Raff auf dich, zu reisen,
Im Flug nur entfliehst du Gewalt und Gesetz.

Im Flug nur entfliehst du der eigenen Schwere,
Die dir dein Wesen umschränkt und erdrückt.
Wirf dich ins Weite, wirft dich ins Leere,
Nur Ferne gewinnt dich dir selber zurück!

Sieh! bloß ein Ruck, und schon rauscht es von Flügeln,
Für dich braust eine eherne Brust,
Heimat stürzt rücklings mit Hängen und Hügeln
Ein Neues, es wird dir neuselig bewußt.

Die Grenzen zerklirren, die gläsernen Stäbe,
Sprachen, die fremden, sie eint dir der Geist
Unendlicher Einheit, da er die Schwebe
Der vierzehn Völker Europas umkreist.

Und in dem Hinschwung von Ferne zu Fernen
Wächst dir die Seele, verklärt sich der Blick,
So wie die Welt im Tanz zwischen Sternen
Schwingend ausruht in großer Musik.

Hymn to the Journey

Rails, the blue veins of iron,
Run across the world, a rushing net.
Heart, run with them! Gather yourself to travel,
Only in flight you escape violence and law.

Only in flight do you escape your own weight,
That restrains and crushes your being.
Throw yourself into space, into emptiness,
Only distance wins your self back!

Look! just a jolt, and it's already rushing from wings,
For you roars a brass breast,
Home crashes backward with slopes and hills
You will know a new one, newly-blessed.

The borders rattle, the glass rods,
For you all foreign languages are united by the spirit
Of unending unity, since it encircles the balance
Of the fourteen peoples of Europe.

And in the outswing from distance to distance
Grows your soul, transfigures the gaze,
As the world in the dance between stars,
Swinging, in great music plays.[1]

---

1 An audio recording of Zweig reading this exists, from 1933.

The Rhythm of New York

A couple of days in this bewildering and, in its strange diversity, both frightening and attractive city. Not long enough to come to terms with it, this city that speaks a hundred languages, that flings together for the first time people from two continents, squalor and wealth parted in a contrast never before seen. I don't understand its voice yet, hardly guess its forms, but already I feel, and in every waking second more strongly, its rhythm, this irresistible, turbulent, excited rhythm of the American metropolis.

For this city is inconceivable as a stable, fixed place, only as movement, as rhythm. We in Europe have cities which are nothing if not the highest form of landscape, which work like music, harmony, a purest, essential concentration of nature reimagined in a human image. Their repose, their being is their beauty. One wishes they always slept, without people, without growth or development, rather brittle, sinking back into timelessness, uninhabited. Florence without tourists or vendors; small German towns, when they're very quiet, with silver moonlight over the sleeping roofs, wonderful in dreamlike, pure, soundless images. The beauty of American cities lies in their reality, in their violence and in the rhythm of their life. They are taunts, violations of nature; but they have the rhythm of the masses, the spirited breath of the people. On Sunday, when this black blood leaves their veins, they're dead, cold, ugly, naked stone quarries, meaningless accumulations of stratified volumes. But weekdays, they ring with a wild beat, with a barbaric, grandiose music, that tones like a song of triumph to the people, testifying with a violence, unknown and terrifying to us, to their swelling vitality. A wonderful life rhythm comes from them. Perhaps here in New York it rings loudest. Since here the New World's outermost edge reaches against the Old World; here the human flood faces each other most wildly. And this rhythm of New York is the first manifestation of the whole American attitude toward life: whoever can feel it understands the high-strained will vibrating in every nerve of this unbounded land.

I first felt this rhythm on Brooklyn Bridge. This gigantic arc— from a distance, a delicate network—that in all its vast masses, startles some on the first day and after a week seems natural, binding two cities of a million people each, like a symbol of solidity. One stands high on the bridge as if on a mountain peak to gauge a wide landscape with wonder. Both right and left is an immense mass of stones with spiky tips, the skyscrapers, sweeping with a murmur of varied noises on both sides. Between them, far below, the wide river, then, in a moment, the bay and the sea. A hunting party of ships trembles: no field is more plowed than this water, ships dig unbroken furrows in the gray tide. From bank to bank ferries call, trains howl against each other, great ocean-going steamships push themselves freely in the wild turmoil. No moment is quiet: like threads being sewed, new ships constantly twitch from the docks, no second without call or answer in these incomprehensible sounds.

One wants to watch all this calmly: but the view is bewildering. On the right, here on the bridge, a train roars by, a second passing over it, an automobile whizzes by on the left, here in the middle of the bridge one stands as if between platforms in a train station. Between storm people, this bridge is railroad, street, highway together, it carries fifty cars a minute, it rings with noise, in the middle of a steep height, arched over the river, one stands on an intersection of ten streets. And it isn't for one second still: one after another, cars tear by as if hoping to smash into each other, while ever more people press back and forth.

Something of a light feeling of dizziness overcomes you. You grasp the railing. And then—this is an odd moment—you feel it: it swings slightly under your hand. You grope at it again. And really, it vibrates; uninterrupted vibration, sometimes stronger, sometimes more weakly, but in the same never-ending rhythm.

From morning to night, from night to morning, this outrageous bridge, whose steel power and force can hardly be described, vibrates like a fine string of human masses, for years it's vibrated like this from the electric voltage of this city. This cord, binding the two million-peopled bunches of New York and Brooklyn like a nerve, quivers constantly in every molecule, and each person up here vibrates with it, from the excitation of the anonymous crowd. Here I felt, for the first time, the rhythm of New York.

1911

Die ferne Landschaft

Sie ist nur ein Traum, von mir als Kind einmal
Vielleicht geträumt, vielleicht sogar erlebt
Auf einer Reise, die ich längst vergaß.

Doch blinkt ihr Bild, als hätte scharfer Stahl
Es losgeschnitten von dem Hintergrund
Der Nacht, nun so in mir: Ein helles Tal,

Das jäh hinabstürzt von der Berge Rund,
Wie wenn es von dem Flusse trinken wollt,
Der lärmend gegen Felsen schmettert und

Dann in die Ferne glitzernd weiterrollt,
Wo reifer Trauben überschattet Blau
Sanft niederfließt in breites Ackergold.

Das Bild ist treu. Ich sehe ganz genau
Aus jedem Traum dieselben Dächer, schräg
Und sonnenwarm, aufatmend fühl ich lau

Des Südens Luft, ich höre von dem Steg
Die Wasser schäumen und seh immer dann
Nach beiden Seiten einen weißen Weg.

Und immer neu rührt mich die Frage an,
Ob ich schon diesen Weg gegangen bin
In Leben oder Traum und wo und wann,

Den weißen Weg, der scheu und zögernd in
Den Rauch der Felsen führt und sanft ins Tal
—Ich weiß es nicht, woher und nicht, wohin —

The Distant Landscape

It's just a dream, that I, as a child,
Maybe dreamed, maybe even lived
On a trip, that I've long forgotten.

But its picture blinks, as if a sharp blade
Cut it from the background
Of night, the same as in me: A bright valley,

Plunging headlong from the mountains' ridge,
As if it wanted to drink from the river,
That bellows noisily against cliffs and

Then into the distance, glistening, rolls on
Where ripe grapes overshadowed blue,
Softly flowing down in wide golden fields.

The picture is recurrent. I see precisely
In each dream the same roofs, sloping
And sun-warmed, sighing I feel the mild

Southern air, I hear from the dock
The waters foaming then always see
On both sides a white path.

And always new the question stirs me,
If I have already taken this path
In life or dream and where and when,

The white path, which shyly and hesitantly in
The smoke of the cliffs leads gently into the valley
— I don't know to or from where —

Und der doch funkelnder als ein Opal
Durch meine Nächte glänzt und bis zum Rand
Sie voll mit Sehnsucht füllt, ein einzig Mal

Auf diesem Weg zu pilgern in ein Land,
Das hinter allen Träumen liegt, so weit
Und wolkenfroh, so fremd und so bekannt,

Als sei es meine eigene Kinderzeit.

And which sparkles more than an opal
Shining through my nights and to the edge
Fills them with longing, just once

On this path to wend my way in a land,
That lies behind all dreams, so distant
And cloud-free, so foreign and known,

As if it were my own childhood.

    1919

Der verlorene Himmel
Elegie der Heimkehrer

Wohin entschwand, der mich noch gestern bestrahlte,
Der rauschende Himmel? Ein Meer, unendlich, umspülte
Er liebend und blau die zackigen Ränder der Erde,
Winde durchfurchten ihn sanft, und lächelnde Wolken
Hellten den ruhenden Ernst zu freundlichem Gruß.
Sterne entblühten ihm nachts wie weiße Zyklamen,
Und der Mond, der uralte Quell aller Träume,
Goß mir kühl aus silbern gebogener Schale
Tröstung ins Herz. Wann immer der Blick, der verwirrte,
Müde des Lands und heiß vom Antlitz der Menschen
Auf zu ihm stieg, ward er begütigt empfangen:
Ewigkeit glänzte ihn an und küßte die Klage,
Die kleinliche, zärtlich fort von dem brennenden Lid.
Selig war ich. Ich glühte, ich blühte nach oben,
Aus allen Wurzeln hob ich mich hoch und verrankte
Unrast und Gier in sein beruhigtes Blau,
Lustvoll spannt' ich mich aus und, selber ein Himmel,
Wölbte sich mir mit heiligen Zeichen die Brust.
Hier, wo ist er, der große, unendlich entspannte?
Zerbrochen hat ihn die Stadt, den Spiegel der Zeiten;
Scherben, zerschellt am gelben Steinbruch der Straßen,
Blinken nur nieder, umdüstert vom Qualm der Fabriken,
Gassen fenstern ihn eng zu grauen Quadraten,
Plätze schleifen ihn rund und, riesige Schrauben,
Bohren die Schorne den wölbigen flach an die Dächer.
Die Sterne ersticken im Dunst, und selten nur eilen
Wolken leichtfüßig durch seinen trüben Morast.
Lehmige Flut, gedämmt vom Felssturz der Straßen,
Schleppt er sich hin, und die aufwärts spähenden Blicke,
Rein sich zu baden an seiner einstigen Reinheit,
Stürzen enttäuscht zurück in das ratlose Herz.

The Lost Sky
The Home-Comers' Elegy

Where did it go, that which yesterday still shone upon me,
The rushing sky? An infinite sea, loving and blue,
It washed around the jagged edges of the earth,
Winds rolled gently through it, smiling clouds
Brightened calm seriousness into a friendly salute.
Stars bloomed in the night sky like white cyclamen,
And the moon, the ancient source of all dreams,
Out of a silver bowed bowl poured
Cool comfort into my heart. Whenever the gaze, confused,
Tired of the country and hot from the face of men,
Turned toward the sky, it was made to feel welcome:
Eternity shone, tenderly kissing away the lament,
The pettiness from the burning eyelid.
Blessed was I. I glowed, I flourished upwards,
I lifted myself up from all my roots, and entwined
Restlessness and greed in its calming blue,
Lustfully, I stretched myself wide, and my chest, a heaven itself,
Swelled with holy signs.
Here, where is it, the wide, infinite sky?
The city has broken it, the mirror of ages;
Smashed by the yellow quarry of the streets,
Shards flash downward, darkened by factory smoke,
Alleys frame it in gray squares,
City squares grind it round and the chimneys, giant screws,
Drill the arched sky flat to the roofs.
Stars choke in the haze, and light-footed clouds
Rarely hurry through its murky morass.
Like a loamy flood, contained by the rock fall of the streets,
The sky drags itself along, and the upward-peering glances
That seek to bathe themselves in its former purity
Crash back, disappointed, into the helpless heart.

Wem hier vertrauen, wem sich aufglühend hingeben,
Da er verdunkelt, der ewige Blick aller Blicke,
Wen frag' ich an? Mit grellgeschminkten Plakaten
Grinsen die Wände, kreischende Lichtbilder hämmern
Sinnlose Worte wie Nägel mir tief im Gedächtnis,
Blicke brennen, Rufe harpunen nach mir.
Alles ist Schrei hier und keiner, mich schweigend zu hören,
Keiner mein Freund. Fieber sind mir die Tage
Ohne den Himmel und dumpf die Stunden der Nacht ohne ihn.
Oh wie schlief ich in seiner unendlichen Wiege!
Weich umhüllte mich Traum, und Summen von Bienen
Bestickte golden die leise tönende Stille,
Winde wiegten mich ein, die Blumen enthauchten
Weihrauch von Duft und machten die Sinne mir fromm.
Atmen hört ich das Land, und die wogenden Brüste
Der Wälder hoben und senkten sich sacht wie die meine.
Nieder fühlt ich mich gleiten vom niederen Strande
Des Tags in tiefere Welt, und waches Besinnen
Löste sich sanft in die freundlich dunkelnde Flut.
Schwärzlich war ich umfangen. Doch unten am Grunde
Glänzten bunt und geschart die Kiesel der Träume,
Arglos nahm ich sie auf, ich rollte die hellen
Und dunkeln in eins, beseligt im kindlichen Spiele,
Bis wieder das Frührot, sanfter Berührung,
Aus den Fingern die leise glitzernden nahm.
Hier, hier stürz ich hinab! Ein eiserner Sarg,
Umpreßt mich der Schlaf.
Über ihn poltern noch schwere Schollen von Lärm,
Mit klirrendem Spatenwurf schaufelt
Mich die fühllose Stadt in den Acker der vielen,
Die hier unter dem irren Kreuzgang der Straßen
Frierenden Blutes daliegen, tot und doch wach.
Immer wühlen noch Stimmen mir nach, und die Häuser
Drücken mir schmerzend mit ihren Steinen die Brust.

Whom can we trust here, to whom should we offer our
    burning passion?
The darkened sky, the eternal gaze of all gazes,
Whom shall I ask? The walls grin with luridly-painted posters,
Screaming light-pictures hammer
Meaningless words like nails deep into my memory,
Looks burn, cries harpoon me.
Everything is scream here and no one to hear me in silence,
None my friend. Without the sky, my days pass in fever
And dull are the hours of the night.
Oh how soundly I slept in its infinite cradle!
Softly enveloped in dreams and the hum of bees,
The soft sounds of silence embroidered in gold.
Rocked by winds, with flowers exhaling incense,
My senses grew pious.
I heard the land breathing, and the billowing breasts
Of the woods lifted and descended gently like my own.
I felt myself gliding down from the low shore of the day
Into a deeper world, and alert thought
Dissolved softly in the friendly darkening flood.
I was caught in darkness. But down at the bottom,
Gathered in shiny piles, shone the pebbles of dreams.
I picked them up innocently, rolling the bright
And the dark ones together, happy in childlike play,
Until the aurora, with a gentle touch,
Took the softly glittering stones from my grasp.
Here, here I fall down! Sleep crushes me
Like an iron coffin.
Heavy clods of noise rain down on it,
From ringing shovels, as the unfeeling city buries me
In the field beneath the mad cloisters of streets
Where so many lie, their blood frozen, dead yet awake.
Voices still dig for me, and the stones of houses
Press painfully against my chest.

Nie verlösch' ich hier ganz. Von Worten und Schreien
Zuckt noch Nachhall in mir, das Kreischen der Schienen
Quert meinen Schlaf, die donnernde Brandung der Wogen
Gischtet ihn an, das wüste Grölen der Trunk'nen,
Röcheln der Kranken, die keuchende Gier der Verliebten,
Angst und Erregung aller, die jetzt noch wach sind,
Sickert in mich und trübt mein dämmerndes Blut.
Auf hohen Türmen hocken schlaflos die Stunden
Und schlagen mit Glocken nach mir. All meine Träume
Dünsten noch Tag und haben die gierigen Blicke
Der Dirnen, die meinen Heimweg abends umstellten,
Angst und Qual von nie gekannten Gelüsten,
Denn viele sind wach noch in mir, indes ich daliege,
Und durch mein Herz stampfen unzählige Schritte,
Fremdes frißt sich mir an und fremde Geschicke
Nisten sich frech in meinen schauernden Schlaf.
Wann, wann hör' ich mich selber, wann tönt der
Seele Musik von hohen Himmel zurück?
Oh ich fühl's, mit ihm, dem selig erhob'nen,
Verlor ich mich selbst. Und mein Herz, das verwirrte,
Schlägt hier nicht eigene Stunde der Brust, sondern hämmert,
Fremd schon sich selbst, den rasenden Rhythmus der Stadt.

I never quite sleep here. The echoes of words and cries
Jerk me awake, the screeching of rails
Crosses my sleep, the thundering surf of the sea
Sprays me with foam, the cawing songs of drunks,
The labored breath of the sick, the panting greed of lovers,
The fear and excitement of all still awake,
Seeps into me and muddies my drowsy blood.
On high towers, the sleepless hours squat
And ring bells for me. All my dreams
Still steam with the day's vapors, with the greedy looks
Of the prostitutes who line my path home in the evening,
The fear and agony of untasted desires,
For many are still awake within me, as I lie here,
And countless footsteps pound through my heart,
Strange things feed on me and strange destinies
Make their brash nests in my shivering sleep.
When, oh when will I hear my own self? When will
The soul's music bounce back from high heaven?
Oh, I feel it, I lost myself to the blessed sky. And my heart,
  confused,
Beats not its own time, but hammers the mad rhythm of the city,
Already a stranger to itself.

Abendliche Flucht

Kennst du das,
Wenn plötzlich – du sitzt bei Schreiben und Sinnen –
Die Wände raunend zusammenrinnen?
Irgendwas
Steht auf und rührt sich in deinem Haus,
Aus den Fenstern starrts, aus den Stühlen sprichts,
Es knarrt auf den Dielen, es blinkert im Glas,
Nichts
Fühlst du als seine Gegenwart.
Und immer enger dringts auf dich ein,
Du fühlst dich umstrickt, du spürst dich umschart.
Und du rufst: es ist deine Stimme nicht.
Was du denkst, ist fremd in dich eingetan,
Fremd starrt dich dein Antlitz im Spiegel an,
Und du schauerst, du weißt nicht mehr, wer du bist,
Nichts ist mehr dein, fremd droht dir das Haus, –
Schatten hält dich umschränkt und beengt,
Bis du, ein Dieb, dir selber entfliehst
Die Treppen hinab, in die Straße hinaus,
Die dich, urbrüderlich Wesen, empfängt
Und wollüstig in ihren Wirbel schwenkt.

Und erst dort, im Gischt ein schwankender Stein,
Fühlst du Rast wieder, Stille und Einsamsein.

Nighttime Flight

Do you know this feeling,
When suddenly —sitting writing and musing —
The walls round you, whispering, seem to be fusing?
Something
Rising up and stirring itself in your house,
Stares in at the windows, speaks from the chairs,
It creaks in the floorboards, flashes at the glass,
You feel
Nothing
But its presence.
And more and more urgently,
You feel ensnared, you feel crowded.
And you call out: it's not your voice.
Your thoughts are alien to you,
Your face in the mirror stares foreignly back,
And you shudder, no longer knowing who you are,
Nothing is yours any longer, the house threatens you strangely, —
Shadow holds you in, restricted and narrow,
Till, like a thief, you flee from yourself
Down the stairs, to the street,
Which receives you, brotherly being,
Lustily sweeping you into its swirl.

And only there, in the spray of a wavering stone,
Do you feel rest again, silence, alone.

1982

MARIA BERL-LEE was born in 1924 in Vienna. At the age of fourteen, she fled to Switzerland alone, eventually rejoining her parents in the south of France. An emergency visa allowed her a passage to New York in 1941. She completed an MA at Fordham University in 1949, and published short stories, poems and plays in both German and English, while working as an interpreter, university instructor and antiquarian. She died in New York 1984.

Manhattan bei Nacht

Rechteck auf Rechteck
        in eintöniger Kongruenz

Werwolfsaugen
        gelbglänzend
        lugen in kalter Neugier
        aus Sarg-Würfeln
die sich schwarz aneinanderreihen
wie ein endloser Trauermarsch

Heulen und klappern
schwerer nachtfarbener Wagen
        Zischen und Dampf
aus eisernen Kratergespenstern
ins Straßenpflaster versenkt

Eine Frau
gleitet hin an leeren Bögen
        verschlossenen Türen
        grell das Gesicht
        dunkel umnebelt ihr Leib
        wissend krächzt ihre Stimme
        Keiner schläft
Eins nach dem anderen
erlöschen die Lichter

Night in Manhattan

Rectangle to rectangle
     in monotonous congruence

Werewolf eyes
     yellow-glittering
     peek in cold curiosity
     from coffin-dice
strung together, black
like an endless mourning march

     Howling and rattling
of heavy night-colored cars
     Hissing and steam
from iron crater ghosts
sunk in pavement

     A woman
glides along empty arches
     closed doors
     her face glaring
     darkness befogs her body
     her voice caws knowingly
     None sleeps
One after the other
the lights go out

Grossstadt-Einsamkeit

Vereinsamt die Straße,
Und die Sonne brennt.
Kein Schall froher Stimmen,
Kein Schritt, den man kennt.

Hoch oben die Stube
Einsam und leer.
Keiner kommt zu Gaste,
Die Zeit wiegt schwer.

Einer Fliege Gebrumm
Am Fenster, eintönig.
Wär mir weniger fremd,
Spräch zu ihr ich ein wenig?

Metropolis Aloneness

The street deserted,
And the sun glows.
No sound of joyous voices,
Not a footstep that you know.

High above, the room
Lonely and empty.
No one visits,
Time weights heavy.

A fly's buzz
At the window, monotone.
If I spoke to it a bit,
Would I feel slightly less alone?

In die Catskills gekommen

Sonnenumzitterte Hügel,
        sanft wie die Mutterbrust
        träumen in blauen Weiten —
fern von Europas Totengebirgen.

Uralter Friede herrscht hier,
wo der Mohawk einsam durch die Ufer zieht
und das Gras noch Siegel trägt
        längstvergangener Stämme.

Kuhglocken tönen feucht-ruhig,
wie die Augen der Tiere,
die grasend nur Frieden wiederkauen.
        Keine Armesünderglocke wimmert.

Du, dem der Tod in den Adern pocht,
bleib stehen mit fliegenden Pulsen:
Schlohweiss gleissen die Farmhäuser
        wie Kindergräber,
wo dein Leben eingescharrt liegt.

Sitzt dir der Tod noch im Nacken?
Vielleicht, in diesen Weiten,
        so gross, so still,
gleitet er sacht zu Boden,
verliert sich im stummen Nicken
        des sensengeweihten
jungen Korns?

In the Catskills

Sun-shaded hills,
        gentle as the mother's breast
        dreaming in blue stretches –
far from Europe's mountains of dead.[1]

Age-old peace reigns here,
where the Mohawk lones across the shores
and the grass still bears seals
        of long-past tribes.[2]

Cowbells sound damp-quiet,
like the eyes of the animals,
which grazing, only ruminate peace.
        No death toll mewls.

You, in whose veins death pumps,
stay standing with flying pulses:
Snow-white gleam the farmhouses
        like childrens' graves,
where your life lies buried.

Does death still sit in your neck?
Maybe, in this vastness,
        so great, so still,
it will glide gently to the ground,
losing itself in the mute nods
        of young grain
destined for the scythe?

---

1 The Toten Gebirge are mountains in the Salzkammergut, used from the
Middle Ages through the eighteenth century for mining and purifying salt, a
process during which they were permanently deforested, thus "dead moun-
tains." Here, the word is a neologism.
2 The word can mean both "tribes" and "tree trunks."

Die weißgetünchte Wohnung in Manhattan

Ich hab' einen Alptraum gehabt
hier in meiner nüchternen
      Wohnung in Manhattan
weißgetüncht, mit allem Komfort,
wo Türhüter und Aufzug
die Mieter
      vor allem Bösen bewahren.

Von der Sintflut hab' ich geträumt
die alles überströmt
      und tötet.
Und ich erwache zu Wasser-Trommeln;
aus der schönvergipsten Decke
taumelt ein Tropenregen,
tröpfelt ein feuchter Fluch.

The Whitewashed Apartment in Manhattan

I had a nightmare
here in my sober
        apartment in Manhattan
whitewashed, with every comfort,
where doorman and elevator
protect the tenants
        from all evil.

I dreamed of the flood
that overflows
        and kills all.
And wake to beating water;
from the beautifully-plastered ceiling
tumbles tropical rain,
trickles a damp curse.

Lament
(original English)

Cold wine
And ashen bread.
If I asked my grieving heart
It would declare me dead.
Pale sun
In a graveyard sky.
It seems small difference that the one
Who died was you, not I.

MIMI GROSSBERG

They Say
(original English)

They say they don't believe that I am dead.
No wonder since they see me move around,
walk back and forth, get up and go to bed
and sing and laugh, and since my skin looks sound.
They say they don't believe that I am dead.
And yet, I'm deader than the death ahead.

ALFRED FARAU was born in Vienna in 1904, where he studied literature, philosophy and pedagogy, then worked as a psychotherapist, produced radio shows, published children's books and novels and, until 1933, wrote for a Berlin newspaper. In 1938 he was sent to Dachau, but with the help of Jewish refugee aid societies, managed to board a ship bound for New York in 1940 with his wife, changing his last name in hopes of protecting his parents as he engaged in antifascist work in America (both Farau's parents, however, died in Auschwitz). Farau found work in a factory, his wife working as a chambermaid, until he managed to find a position again as a psychotherapist. He became a member of the New York Academy of Sciences, and was eventually awarded an Austrian honorary professorship before dying in New York in 1972. An uncompleted project begun in his later years was a dramatic work on Native American societies and psychology.

Die Rettung

Und eines Tages war die Flucht zu Ende,
an neuen Ufern fand ich mich, gerettet.
Gerettet? — nur noch unlösbarer bin ich
mit jenen drüben schicksalshaft verkettet.

Kann der gerettet sein, dem immerwährend
das grenzenlose Leid vor Augen steht,
der überdauern muss, wie Stück für Stück
von seiner Welt versinkt und untergeht? !

So wie Odysseus in des Riesen Höhle
selbst noch den Schlaf der Teuersten bewacht,
mit jedem Pulsschlag das Entsetzen spürend
und unerbittlich schau'n muss Tag und Nacht;

so wie der Gläubige den Blick nach Mekka
nicht nur im täglichen Gebete nimmt,
— wie dieses Ziel zuletzt sein ganzes Wesen
von innen her beleuchtet und bestimmt;

so hat auch alles, was ich tu und treibe,
nur EINEN Sinn noch, SINN von ihrem Leben,
darf ich nur atmen mehr und weiterkämpfen,
an ihren Abgrund schaudernd hingegeben,

steh ich in jedem Lebensaugenblicke
vor ihrem Jammer, ihrer Not geneigt:
in einer Qual, die alles überbietet,
in einer Scham, die nichts mehr übersteigt.

The Rescue

And one day flight came to an end,
on new shores I found myself, rescued.
Rescued? — I am only more insolubly
chained by fate to those over there.

Can he be rescued, before whose eyes
the borderless suffering forever stands,
who must endure, as piece by piece
his world sinks and collapses? !

Like Odysseus in the giant's cave
even guards the sleep of the dearest,
feeling horror with every pulse
and must be inexorably on guard day and night;

as the believer turns his gaze toward Mecca
not only in daily prayer,
— like this goal at last his whole being
illuminates and determines from the inside;

so everything I do has
just ONE sense, SENSE of their lives,
may I just breathe and keep fighting,
shuddering at their abyss, devoted,

I stand in every moment of life
in the face of their misery, bowed toward their distress:
in a torment that surpasses everything,
in a shame that cannot be exceeded.

FRANCISCO TANZER, born in 1921 in Vienna, fled to Paris in 1938 (where he attended high school), to Lisbon in 1940, and to New York in 1941. From 1942-1947 he served in the US Army, and was deployed to Germany. In 1947 he returned to New York to study, then worked with Voice of America. Moving to Germany in 1954, he became involved in writing for film and television, dying in Düsseldorf in 2003. He published a novel and short stories. His poetry has been set to music by, among others, Alfred Schnittke, Sofia Gubaidulina, and John Cage.

Später einmal ...

Rot-braun	Rot-braun	Rot-braun
Schimmert	Schimmert	Schimmert
Dein Haar	Dein Haar	Dein Haar
In der	In der	In der
Sonne	Sonne	Sonne
Des Frühlings	Des Frühlings	Des Frühlings
Und ich	Und ich	Und ich
Frag mich	Frag mich	Frag mich
Wie später	Wie später	Wie später
Einmal	Einmal	Einmal
Das Leben	Die Liebe	Das Leben
Es kämmt	Es nennt	Uns trennt
Frag mich	Frag mich	Frag mich
Vergebens	Vergebens	Vergebens
Weil die	Weil jeder	Weil die
Grenze	Seine	Grenze
Des eigenen	Eigene	Der eigenen
Lebens	Liebe	Liebe
Mich hemmt	Nur kennt	Mich hemmt

Someday Later . . .

Red-brown	Red-brown	Red-brown
Gleams	Gleams	Gleams
Your hair	Your hair	Your hair
In the	In the	In the
Springtime	Springtime	Springtime
Sun	Sun	Sun
And I	And I	And I
Ask myself	Ask myself	Ask myself
As later	As later	As later
Someday	Someday	Someday
Life	Love	Life
Will comb it	It calls	Separates us
Ask myself	Ask myself	Ask myself
In vain	In vain	In vain
Since the	Since each	Since the
Border	Their	Border
Of my own	Own	Of my own
Life	Love	Love
Hems me in	Only knows	Hems me in

GERTRUDE URZIDIL was born near Prague in 1898. A childhood friend of Franz Kafka and member of the Prague Literary Circle, she published poetry, essays and "prose studies of famous women." In 1939, she fled through Italy to England, then in 1941 to New York, where she worked as a nanny, taking US citizenship in 1946. She died in New York in 1977.

Grosses Geschick

Ein Herzstück blieb in Prag zurück.
In Amerika leb ich auf Reisen.
Das steigert den Alltag zu grossem Geschick,
er bewegt sich in neuen Geleisen.

Die Kindheit meldet sich wieder zu Wort:
Lerne lesen, schreiben und gehen!
Dann wirst du auch am fernsten Ort
die Proben der Fremde bestehen.

Great Skill

A part of the heart stayed behind in Prague,
In America I'm just travelling.
That raises daily life to a great skill,
it moves along new tracks.

Childhood memories speak up once more:
Learn to read, to write, and to stand!
Then you will, even on the furthest shore,
pass the tests of the foreign land.

Fragen eines Kindes

Ich sah in der Untergrundbahn ein Kind,
das verstand es noch, seine Fahrt zu genießen.
Es fragte laut, wer die Zauberer sind,
die alle Türen öffnen und schließen.

Melden sie uns auch die Stationen?
Wissen sogar die nächste voraus?
Wo nur die guten Geister wohnen?
Hier, in dem Zug, oder in einem Haus?

Lenken sie auch die rollende Stiege,
welche uns wieder zur Straße bringt?
Das Märchen der Kindheit erzählt keine Lüge,
da es den frühen Alltag besingt.

A Kid's Questions

I saw a kid in the subway,
who still knew how to enjoy his ride.
He shouted to know what magicians
closed and opened the doors wide.

Is it they who call out the stations?
Knowing the next before it arrives?
But where do they live, the good spirits?
Here in the train, or outside?

Do they also move the steps
that bring us back up to the street?
Childhood's fairy tale tells no lie,
as it sings of young everyday life.

Zinshaus tief in Queens

Auf der Insel, die sich Walt Whitmans rühmt,
sind wir eines Hauses hundertachtzigste Partei.
Man grüßt einander, wie es sich ziemt,
nur selten geht jemand wortlos vorbei.

Es ist besser, wenn man mit anderen wohnt,
als die Welt zu messen nach seinem Gartenbeet.
Von den hundertachtzig Arten Lärm bleibt niemand verschont.
Aber man fühlt sich nicht als Mitte, um die sich alles dreht.

Keines der Kinder hier ist ohne Gespielen,
sepiafarbig, gelb, schwarz und weiß.
Groß sind die Knaben, die mit Bällen gut zielen;
groß sind die Mädchen, die flink sind im Kreis.
Wenn man da ihre Rufe durchs Fenster hört,
zu jeder Jahreszeit und immer beschwingt,
glaube keiner, der gute graue Barde fühle sich gestört,
denn er ist's ja, der den Kindern von den Grashalmen singt.

Apartment House Deep in Queens

On the island which prides itself on Walt Whitman,
we are a building's one-hundred-eightieth tenants.
Greeting each other, as it befits,
rarely does someone go by without words.

It's better to live with others,
than to measure the world from one's garden plot.
No one is spared from the hundred-and-eighty kinds of noise.
But one feels not like the center, around which all revolves.

No child here's without playmates,
sepia-toned, yellow, black and white.
Great are the boys who aim balls well,
great are the girls who ring in a circle.[1]
When you hear their calls from the window,
in every season, and always bright,
no one believes the good gray bard is annoyed,
for it's he who sings to the children of leaves of grass.

---

1 Likely a reference to Whitman's "Great are the Myths" from *Leaves of Grass*.

FRANZI ASCHER-NASH, daughter of the composer Leo Ascher, was born in Vienna in 1910, studied singing, was a choral singer in the Vienna Volksoper, and published short stories in Viennese newspapers. In 1938, she fled to New York, where she worked as a secretary, translator, and librarian. She wrote short radio plays for the "Freie Deutsche Radiostunde," published articles on daily life in the United States in the *Austro American Tribune*, and lectured on music at the New School for Social Research. She died in Lancaster, PA in 1992.

Sommernacht

Es ist nichts Böses, ist ja nur die Hitze,
daß ich nicht schlafen kann in dieser langen Nacht,
und daß mir ist, als hingen neue Blitze
im Finstern, und als stünde niemand Wacht.

Als wären ohne Antwort alle Hände,
als stünden schwarze Mauern um uns her,
als wären alle Wege längst zu Ende
in einem stummen, blinden, regungslosen Meer.

Da fühl' ich, wie mein Atem plötzlich anhält:
ein Auto fährt vorbei – nein! Es kehrt um!
Und wie die alte Angst mich wieder anfällt –
denn nachts geht drüben die Vernichtung um.

Die Aufzugtüre kreischt und Schritte kommen näher
und immer näher . . . ist die Tür versperrt?
Und ist sie's auch, der braune Griff der Späher
hat schon aus tausend Türen Opfer vorgezerrt.

Da erklingt ein gläsern leises Klirren,
hell und zart, wie Botschaft und Gewähr:
Es war der Milchmann. Laß dich nicht verwirren.
Jene Hand reicht nicht bis übers Meer.

Und am Gang verklingt der Schritte leises Hämmern,
aufgeschluckt vom Rinnen dunkler Zeit,
vor den Fenstern aber steht das erste Dämmern,
und ich weiß, der Tag ist nicht mehr weit.

1939

Summer Night

It's nothing bad, it's just the heat,
that I can't sleep in this long night,
and that it seems to me as if new lightning beat
in the dark, and as if no one stood watch.

As if all hands had no answer,
as if black walls stood around us,
as if all paths were long ended
in a silent, blind, motionless sea.

That's when I feel my breath stop suddenly:
a car drives by — no! It's turning around!
And how the old fear again overtakes me—
since, over there, it's at night that annihilation sounds.

The elevator door shrieks and steps come closer
and ever closer . . . is the door locked?
And even if so, the watchman's brown grip
has already pulled victims from thousands of doors.

There a glassy clang sounds,
bright and tender, as message and guarantee:
It was the milkman. Don't get confounded.
That hand doesn't reach across the sea.

And in the corridor, the footsteps faintly hammer away,
swallowed up by the pour of dark hours,
but at the windows hangs the first light of day,
and I know the dawn is no longer far.

1939

FRIDERIKE MARIA ZWEIG, born in Vienna in 1882, wrote biographies, novels, and poetry. While working as a newspaper journalist, she met and married Stefan Zweig in 1912. The couple separated in 1938, but both fled to New York in 1940. As refugee quotas for the year were full, Friderike entered the United States with a tourist visa and, two years later, crossed into Canada and back, reentering with a longer-stay visa. In 1943 she founded the Writers Service Center in New York City for refugee authors, and helped found the American-European Friendship Association the same year. She died in Stamford, CT in 1971.

Traum im Winter

Es steht vereinzelt in des Nachbarn Garten
Ein Lärchenbaum, recht selten hierzulanden.
Ich denk an die, die dicht zusammenstanden
Im fernen Lärchenwald in Tirol.

Die Lärchen lassen ihre Nadeln fallen
Zur Winterzeit im rauhen kalten Norden.
So ist mein Baum hier kahl und nackt geworden
Wie die im fernen Lärchenwald in Tirol.

Doch dieser winterliche Baum,
Den ich stets grüsse im Vorübergehen,
Erweckt in mir verscholl'nen Traum
Vom fernen Lärchenwald in Tirol.

Winter Dream

Standing alone in the neighbor's yard
Is a larch tree, right rare to find here.
I think on those bunched together near
In the distant larch woods in Tyrol.

The larches let their needles fall
In winter time in the harsh cold North.
My tree, too, has become naked and bald
Like those in the distant larch woods in Tyrol.

So this wintry tree,
Which I greet each time I pass by,
Awakens a forgotten dream in me
Of the distant larch woods in Tyrol.[1]

---

1 One of the last poems Zweig wrote before her death.

NORBERT GROSSBERG was born in 1903 in Vienna, and worked as an optometrist and traveling salesman. He fled with his wife Mimi to New York in 1938, formed a small performing group called "See New York First" (a play on "See America First") and published articles in newspapers and anthologies, and a volume of poetry. He died in New York in 1970.

Central Park Hypertrophien

Im Central Park stehen die Bäume auf teuerem Grund
und zahlen Miete für Platz, Wasser und Licht.
Ihre Blätter rauschen die letzten
Nachrichten der Stunde
in den Sprachen der fünfzig
Nationen der Stadt.
Im Teiche tauchen die schönsten
Mädchen der Welt,
um Fische zu fangen für
die zahlenden Millionäre
und das Ergebnis der "Show"
fließt in die Taschen des
Komitees zum Schutze der
Frauenarbeit am Nordpol.
In elektrisch betriebenen Kinderwagen
liegen die Babies der Reichen
eingeschläfert vom "Sing-Sing-Song"
der Colt-bewaffneten Bonnen,
träumend vom kühnsten der Gangster,
leise flüsternd als erstes der Worte: "Al Capone!"

Im Zoo, nicht weit davon,
schüttelt ein sex-appealender Löwe
seine dauergewellte Mähne und zerkaut
mit gold-plombierten Zähnen
Corned Beef von Armour & Swift.
Die Vögel in der Voliére
tragen federngeschmückte Hüte,
die den "dernier cri de la mode"
weit überflügeln . . .
Und ein Papagei, heiser vor Wut,
krächzt ständig ins Mikrophon,

Central Park Hypertrophies

In Central Park the trees stand on expensive land
and pay rent for space, water and light.
Their leaves rustle the lastest
news of the hour
in the languages of the city's
fifty nations.
In the pond dive the prettiest
girls in the world,
to catch fish for
the paying millionaires
and the funds from the "show"
flow to the pockets of the
committee for the protection of
women's work at the North Pole.
In electric-propelled strollers
lie the babies of the rich
lullabyed by the "Sing-Sing-song"
of Colt-armed nannies,
dreaming of the wildest of gangsters,
softly whispering their first word: "Al Capone!"

In the zoo, not far away,
a lion with sex appeal
shakes his permed mane
chewing Armour & Swift corned beef
with gold-plated teeth.
The birds in the aviary
wear feathered hats
that far outstrip
the *dernier cri de la mode* . . .
And a parrot, hoarse with fury,
croaks constantly into the microphone,

zum Sit-down-strike aufhetzend,
die Fünf-Tage-Woche fordernd
für den Besuch des Zoos,
um den Tieren endlich zwei Ruhetage zu sichern.

Und ich schrieb dies an einem Julitag
bei 115 Grad Fahrenheit,
als die Thermometerröhre platzte
und ihr Inhalt in zierlichen Kaskaden
herauszuspringen begann
und kann, was ich alles erblickte,
noch immer nicht ganz begreifen . . .

inciting sitdown strikes,
demanding five-day weeks
for visiting the zoo,
to finally give the animals two days off.

And I wrote this on a July day
of 115 degrees,
as the thermometer burst
and its contents in dainty cascades
began leaping out
and can, of everything I saw,
still not completely understand it all . . .

Times Square um Mitternacht

Da Tausende Theater und Kinos verließen,
Ist der Times Square jetzt die große Bühne.
Das Publikum spielt sich selbst.
Wir üben Kritik an jedermanns[1] Miene.
Hotels, Bars und Kitschläden sind die Kulissen.
Die Menge wälzt sich, stoßend und drängend.
Die Neonlampen, die das Bild erhellen,
bringen Reklamebotschaften ans Licht,
Cartoons laufen an vielen Stellen,
Tages-Geschichte erzählt der Times News-Reel,
gibt sachlich und nüchtern Bericht
in wechselndem Glühlampenspiel.
Ich begegne menschlichen Vergangenheiten
und Silhouetten sonder Zahl,
verglaster Stumpfheit, Mädchenblicken, die rühren,
Gestalten, noch träumend von Rauschseligkeiten.
Worte flackern, ohne Schall,
die niemals zu Gesprächen führen.
Es schrillen Pfiffe, Autohupen dröhnen,
der Tod,[2] verleidet, sitzt am Steuerrad,
die Kappe tief in seine Stirn geschoben,
und seine Tagesbeute hör' ich stöhnen –
und Lust und Gier, sie formen ein Quadrat,
zur furchtbarsten Potenz erhoben.
Schallplatten schrillen Liebeslieder,
die Nadel geht jetzt auf den Strich.[3]
Im Tunnel unten fährt die automatisierte Bahn,
rennt ohne Passagiere hin und wieder.
Ein Mann, den Stadtplan in der Hand,
sieht sich das staunend an.
Ein Kind, allein, malt Männchen an die Wand.

---

1 Also, a character in the Austrian play *Jedermann*, based on a fifteenth-century
English morality play.
2 Another character from the same play.
3 Also, in German, red light district.

Times Square at Midnight

As thousands leave theaters and cinemas,
Times Square is now the main stage.
The audience plays itself.
We exchange critiques of anyone's face.
Hotels, bars and kitsch shops are the backdrops.
The crowd waltzes, pushing and shoving.
The neon lights that light the scene
bring advertising messages to light
cartoons play on many a screen,
daily news is told by the Times news reel,
gives a sober and matter-of-fact report
in changing light bulb play.
I encounter human pasts
and silhouettes without number,
glassy dullness, girls' gazes, stirring
characters still blissfully dreaming.
Words flicker, without sound,
never leading to conversations.
Whistles whistle, car horns drone,
death, disgusted, sits at the wheel,
cap pushed low on his forehead,
and I hear his day's prey moan —
and lust and greed, they form a square,
raised to the most fearful potency.
Vinyl records shrill love songs,
the needle rides now to the locked groove.
In the tunnel below runs the automated train,
runs without riders now and again.
A man, city map in hand,
looks on, enthralled.
A lone child paints little men on the wall.

Metropolis

Ein schlafendes, unheimlich träumendes
vielgliedriges Fabelwesen lag an den Ufern
der beiden Wasserwege: glühend mit tausend Lichtern,
die nervös zuckten, tönend aus Mikrophonen,
Lokomotiven, Autohupen, echowerfenden Tunneln,
zehn Millionen kreischenden schreienden, betenden,
flehenden Menschenkehlen, drohenden, zischenden
Dampfturbinen, schrillen Möwenschreien, Elevator-
schienen-Klirren; tausend verschiedene Düfte aus-
strömend aus Blumenkisten, Schornsteinen, Küchen,
Fleisch-, Gemüse- und Obstmärkten, aus Alkoholboutiquen,
Öltankern, Benzinbehältern, Kanälen, Proviantabfällen
von Schiffen; mit blinden Autofriedhofsaugen, Fisch-
starren Brillen, glitzernden Menschenaugen, Katzen-
leuchten, Tränen; Stöhnen aus Rauschgiftgesichtern,
strahlenden und geschminkten, girrenden, lockenden,
bittenden, flehenden, drohenden, demütig sich
anbietenden, anheimelnden, abstoßenden; häßliche,
schmutzige, karbolausströmende Wundverbände; Hafen,
Hölle, Zuflucht, Asyl, Kerker, Ewigkeitsbahnhof;
gleichgültig, verheißend, verschlingend und
beschützend, zermalmend und vergessend, lebend
und sterbend, verbrennend, erneuernd, verfaulend
und sprießend, unbegreiflich, überwältigend,
hoffnungsvoll, trostlos, dollarklirrend, um Pennies
bettelnd, Gebrechen zeigend, Sportsgestalten und
Priester, Primitivität neben Glanzpunkten der Technik;
kapitalistische Hochburg und rattenverseuchte Slums,
Anarchismus und Vereinte Nationen; seelenloses
Riesentier, zugleich schüchtern Anerkennung erbittend;
so wollte es auch mich verschlingen oder erhöhen;
es ist ein endloses Ringen, wer wen besiegen wird.
Noch leben wir beide – haßliebend.

Metropolis

A sleeping, uncannily dreaming
multi-faceted mythical creature lay on the banks
of both waterways: glowing with a thousand nervously twitching
lights, ringing from microphones,
locomotives, car horns, echoing tunnels,
ten million shrieking, screaming, praying,
pleading human throats, menacing, hissing
steam turbines, shrill seagull cries, elevated-
rails-clank; a thousand different smells pour-
ing from flower boxes, chimneys, kitchens,
meat-, vegetable- and fruit-markets, from liquor stores,
oiltankers, gasoline tankers, canals, food waste
from ships; with blind auto junkyard eyes, fish-
staring glasses, glittering human eyes, cat-
flashes, tears; moaning from drugged faces,
radiant and made-up, grating, alluring,
pleading, imploring, threatening, humbly offering
themselves, homely, repellent; ugly,
dirty, carbolic acid leaking wound dressings; port,
hell, refuge, asylum, dungeon, eternal train station;
indifferent, promising, devouring and
protective, crushing and forgetting, living
and dying, burning, renewing, rotting
and sprouting, ungraspable, overwhelming,
hopeful, hopeless, dollar-jangling, begging
for pennies, ailment-showing, sports figures and
priests, primitiveness beside highlights of technology;
capitalistic fortress and rat-infested slums,
anarchism and United Nations; soulless
great beast, simultaneously timidly requesting recognition;
it wanted to devour or raise me up, too;
this is an endless wrestle, who beats who.
So we both still live — hate-loving.

ERNST WALDINGER, born outside Vienna in 1896, was partially paralyzed by injuries received as a soldier in the First World War. While still in an intensive care unit, he enrolled to study art history and German literature in Vienna, completing a doctoral degree, working for a newspaper, publishing his first poetry in 1924, and co-founding the Socialist Writer's Union, which Austria outlawed in 1934. Most of his papers were destroyed. Because his wife, a niece of Sigmund Freud, had been born in the United States, the couple was able to escape Austria in 1938 for New York, where Waldinger worked in a retail store, as a librarian, and finally as a professor of German literature at Skidmore College in Saratoga Springs. He co-founded the Aurora Press, which published Austrian authors in exile and was, after the war, awarded literary prizes in Austria. Waldinger died in New York City in 1970.

Ein Pferd in der 47. Straße

Es regnet, und ein Strom vom Schirmen zieht.
Fifth Avenue und Forty-seventh Street.

Um Mittag spein die Tore Schar um Schar:
Nach Gummimänteln riecht das Trottoir;

Nach feuchtem Müll die Straße, nach Benzin;
Verkehrskolonnen hupen drüber hin;

Nun halten sie; im nassen Asphalt schaut
Ein Autochaos spiegelnd sich und staut

Sich, starr, als ob es eingefroren sei:
Das grüne Licht gibt mir die Straße frei.

Von Menschenwogen werd ich mitgeschwemmt –
Da stock ich jäh, denn irgendwas ist fremd;

Inmitten der Mechanik Segensfluch,
Riech ich vergeßnen, guten Roßgeruch:

Wahrhaftig, zwischen Autos ragt ein Gaul,
Mit plumpen Hufen, ruhelosem Maul.

Hat er mir nicht soeben zugenickt?
Mit müden Augen so mich angeblickt,

Als ständ zu fragen dumpf in seinem Sinn:
Bist du so einsam hier, wie ich es bin?

A Horse in 47th Street

It's raining, and a river of umbrellas meet.
Fifth Avenue and Forty-seventh Street.

At noon doors spit out throngs wearing galoshes:
The sidewalk smells of mackintoshes;

The street of damp trash, of gasoline;
Rows of traffic honk in the thick stream;

Now they pause; in damp asphalt
A motored chaos sees itself reflected, halts

As if frozen, rigid, freezing for a beat:
The green light gives me access to the street.

Swept along by waves of men so many —
I stop short, as something's most uncanny;

In the midst of the mechanic's blessing-curse,
A whiff of the forgotten, good old smell of horse:

It's true — a horse stands mid the autos' muddle,
With clumsy hooves and restless muzzle.

Did he not just nod at me as I did at him likewise?
Like me toward him he gazed with tired eyes,

As if the question stood dully in his mind:
Are you as lonely here as I?

1938

Nachts am Hudson

Noch eben rollte er im breiten Schwall
Aus glühendem Abendgold, flankiert von Klippen
Und Fensterreihn; umglittert von den Rippen
Der Türme fingen sie den Sonnenball.

Nun ist es Nacht; er kollert Widerhall
Von Zügen, untergrund; und Krane kippen
Mit Golem-Armen; wie von Fieberlippen
Stöhnt einer Schiffssirene dumpfer Schall.

Und doch, wie ich im Grase sinnend lieg,
Fließt nun der dunkle Strom an mir vorbei,
Als ob's noch in der Urwaldlandschaft sei:

Kein Großstadt-Dschungel, kein Maschinenkrieg!
In ewig-unentzifferbaren Sigeln
Seh ich die Sterne sich im Wasser spiegeln.

Night on the Hudson

Just rolling in a wide swell
Of glowing evening gold, flanked by cliffs
And rows of windows; glittering ribs
Of the towers caught the sun.

Now it's night; it reverberates
With trains, underground; and cranes tilt
With Golem-arms; as from fevered lips
A ship's siren groans its dull sound.

And then, as I lie musing in the grass,
The dark stream flows past,
As if still in the jungle landscape:

No metropolis-jungle, no machine-war!
In eternally indeterminable outlines
I see the stars reflected in the water.

Der Wolkenkratzer

Wenn in den Häusergebirgen, in den Klippen,
Um die der Maelstrom der Tumulte brandet,
Von Stock zu Stock der Aufzug tost und landet,
Wenn in den Menschenstöcken, in den Stahlgerippen
Mit tausend Kojen in Beton gewandet,
Vom Tor bis zu des höchsten Turmes Kupferknauf,
Um den die Chöre der Sirenen brüllen,
In Korridoren, die sich hastig füllen,
Die Fieberkurve, der gehetzte Lauf
Sich selber hetzt – o losgelaßne Hölle,
Wo die Arbeit überkocht, als quölle
Die ganze Gier des Universums auf . . .

Dies ist ein Traum, phantastisch wie ein Traum,
Wenn die Giganten sich des Nachts erhellen,
Türme mit tausend strahlenden Kerkerzellen,
In Licht ertrinkend, daß der weiße Schaum
Aus allen Poren spritzt von den Fassaden
In Fällen rauscht, in zuckenden Kaskaden,
Unrast ist Licht geworden, Glanz ist Hast,
Verheißungsvoller, gleißend-toller Glast,
Mit Strömen von Begehrlichkeit geladen;
Licht tobt, Licht blendet, grell geschminkte Pracht,
Licht geißelt sich mänadisch durch die Nacht.

Die Wanderschrift am fünften Stockwerk brennt
Mit roten Riesenlettern, atemlos
Brennt sie die Sensationen in den Schoß
Der Dunkelheit, rotiert und rast und rennt
Mit riesig-roten Lettern, wird verschluckt
Und fängt von neuem an – ein Viadukt,
Der seinen Bogen über Schluchten schnellt,

The Skyscraper

When in the house-mountain-ranges, in the cliffs,
Around which the turmoil's maelstrom surges,
From floor to floor the elevator roars and purges,
When in the human hives, in the steel ribs
With a thousand berths that concrete submerges,
From the entrance to the highest copper tower,
Round which the choirs of sirens roar,
In quickly-filling corridors,
The rushing run, the fevered sweep,
Hounds itself—oh liberated Hell,
Where the work overcooks, while swells
Up the universe's whole greed . . .

This is a dream, fantastic as a dream,
When the giants light themselves up at night,
Towers with a thousand dungeon cells so bright,
Drowning in light, which the white gleam
From every pore shoots from the façades
In cases rushing, in twitching cascades,
Unrest has become light, radiance is haste,
Enchanting, glittering-great glass,
Laden with streams of greediness;
Garishly made-up grandeur, raging light, dazzling light,
Light mauls itself, Maenad-like, through the night.

The scrolling text on the fifth floor burns
With giant red letters, breathless
Burn the sensations in darkness's
Lap, races and runs and turns
With huge red letters, inward sucked
And starts anew—a viaduct,
Shooting its arc over ravines,

Saust knapp vorüber, Hochbahnzüge blitzen,
Daß die Fenster wie die Funken ineinanderflitzen,
Und herab vom Restaurant des Daches schellt
Das Schlagwerk aus dem Kapellenlärm, verloren
Im Lärm der donnernden Autobusmotoren.

Dies ist ein Traum, phantastisch wie ein Traum,
Dein Blick stürzt ab, wenn er zur Höhe klimmt,
Die Augen stolpern, und verflirrend schwimmt
Die Linie der Firste durch den Raum;
Ein Schwindel mengt die rasenden Mäander
Von hunderten Geschossen durcheinander,
Und alles scheint zu taumeln, wächst ins Wirre,
Verkehrt sich und verzerrt sich, führt ins Irre,
Und scheint bis ins Unendliche zu ragen;
Die Fronten weichen wankend nach der Seite,
Als wollten sie mit ungeheurer Breite
Den Himmel auf der flachen Plattform tragen.

Du stehst zu nah, so faßt du nur die Angst
Beseßnen Wildes, das sich selber treibt.
Des Jägers Furcht, der der Gejagte bleibt,
Wenn du ins Weite und zur Schau gelangst,
Dann wird die Zahl, mit Zahlen nicht zu stillen,
Des bloße Durst, nur um des Durstes willen,
Der selbst sich anspringt, seiner Seele Mord,
Das blinde Mehr, der Wahnwitz, der Rekord,
Die Wollust, die sich an die Wolken rafft,
Der Krampf von heute wird einmal die Kraft,
Der Zukunft Samen und vertausendfältigt:
Wer fluchend kam, steht staunend überwältigt.

Just beyond flash elevated trains' marks,
Their windows streaking past each other like sparks,
And down from the roof-top restaurant rings
The percussion from the chapel noise, lost
In the ruckus from thundering bus engines tossed.

This is a dream, fantastic as a dream,
Your gaze plummets as it climbs to the rim
The eyes stumble and, baffled, swim
In space roofs float in a stream;
A dizziness fills the raging meander
Shot from hundreds pell-mell,
And everything seems to stagger, grows to confusion,
Turns and distorts itself, leads to delusion,
And seems to extend ad infinitum;
Façades sway softly side to side,[1]
As if they wanted, tremendous, wide
To carry the sky on the flat podium.

You stand too close, so you only fear
Wild creatures, self-propelled.
The hunter's fear that he himself is hunted,
If you go far in the distance and near,
Then the number, by numbers unsated,
Sheer thirst, for thirst's sake unslaked,
Who starts himself, his soul murder,
The blind More, the madness, the record,
The lust rafting to the clouds' brink,
The cramp of today will be the strength,
That seeds the future thousand-fold:
He who cursing came, stands astonished, over-bowled.

---

1 "Fronts" in German can mean a line of buildings, but more commonly
refers to the front ranks of an army.

ALFRED GONG was born in Czernowitz (today Chernivtsi, in western Ukraine) in 1920, and was a schoolmate of Paul Celan. While studying literature at the University of Czernowitz in 1939, he was expelled when the Soviet Union annexed the city, not because his family was Jewish, but because it was upper-middle class. His parents and sister were caught by a police raid and sent to Siberia while he happened to be sleeping over at a friend's house. He became a village schoolteacher, but when Germany invaded Russia, he was deported to a ghetto in Moldavia in 1941, this time not for being bourgeois, but for being Jewish. He escaped, living in hiding in Bucharest with friends and writing film reviews for the "Aryanized" press under a pen name. When it became the clear the Iron Curtain was closing in 1946, he took a "business trip" to Vienna and never returned, publishing in a small literary circle in Vienna from 1946-1950, then moving to the United States in 1951, to work in a factory, then as a waiter, translator and social worker. He published stories, essays and poems, including "Happening in der Park Avenue," and the anthology "Interview mit Manhattan." In 1966 he was awarded a Theodor Körner Prize, and died in the United States in 1981.

USA

Auf den Atlanten
an die Haut eines Bisons
gemahnend, vom Großen Trapper
zum Trocknen gespannt
zwischen beiden Ozeanen,
die von diesen Küsten zehren
mit ihren Gezeiten aus Salz
und dem sangre azul
aller Konquistadoren.

Welch Gewimmel
um dieses Festland!
Zwischen Boje und Bohrturm:
Spuren der Mayflower,
Moby Dick und Nautilus –
gewiegt vom Atem der Brandzug
und von den Synkopen der Zeit.

Darüber, am rastlosen Himmel:
die Keile der Ornis, die Schwärme
der Jets, vertraut mit den Straßen
zwischen Weizen und Wüste,
versöhnt mit Firn und Feuer,
zugetan den Narben der Ströme
und Kardiogrammen des Marktes,
gewöhnt an skalpierte Gebirge,
an Türme, Antennen-bewaldet,
verbunden den Kreisen, geätzt
ins Relief dieser Breitwand –

Kladde verwichener Götter,
Labor der Götter von morgen.

USA

On the atlases
reminiscent of the skin of a bison
stretched to dry
by the great trapper
between both oceans,
which feed on these coasts
with their salt tides
and the blue blood
of all conquistadors.

What a bustle
about this land!
Between buoy and derrick:
traces of the Mayflower,
Moby Dick and Nautilus —
rocked by the breath of fires of war
and by the fainting of time.

Above, in the restless sky:
the thrashing of the native birds, swarms
of jets, familiar with the streets
between wheatfields and desert,
reconciled with snow and fire,
attached to the scars of the rivers
and cardiograms of the stock market,
familiar with scalped mountains,
with antenna-forested towers,
bound with the circles, etched
in the relief of this silver screen —[1]

Notepad of drowned gods,
Lab of the gods of tomorrow.

---

1 *Breitwand* can be either a cinema screen or the face of a mountain.

Manhattan Spiritual

Männlein und Weiblein Manhattans,
helfen Couch und Pillen euch nicht,
schlagt dann in der Bibel nach,
sie weist euch den Weg ins Licht.

Adam, verbleu deine Rippe
samt Apfel und Feigenblatt.
Noah, mix den Martini:
wir haben das Wasser satt.
Josua, blas in dein Blechhorn:
Stahl und Glas, sie stürzen nicht ein.
Jonas, kriech aus dem U-Boot
und kehr ZUM WALFISCH ein.

Im Neubabel Manhattan
lärmt's in allen Zungen der Welt,
doch beredter als Zungen
schweigt hier und spricht das Geld.

Jakob, vergiß deine Leiter,
der Aufzug führt rascher zum Ziel:
Rachel hat schönere Beine,
Lea mehr Geld und Profil.
Kain, wirf fort deine Waffe,
Hände hoch und komm brav heraus.
Wer möchte Klein Moses adoptieren?,
z. Z. im Findelhaus.

In den Sendern Manhattans
singen Engel mit Sirup-Sopran.
Ein gefallener Engel
schnarcht in der Untergrundbahn.

Manhattan Spiritual

Man and woman of Manhattan,
the couch and the pills offer no aid,
so go have a look in the Bible,
and let it light your way.

Adam, bash your rib
along with the fig leaf and apple.
Noah, mix the martini:
we've had water enough, quite ample.
Joshua, blow your horn:
Steel and glass, they won't fall.
Jonah, come out of the submarine
and go TO THE WHALE.

In the new Babel Manhattan
sound all the world's tongues in riot,
but more eloquent than tongues
money speaks here and keeps quiet.

Jacob, forget your ladder,
the elevator gets you there quicker:
Rachel has prettier legs,
Leah more money and profile.
Cain, throw down your weapon,
hands up and now come out.
Who wants to adopt little Moses?,
Available now in the foundling house.

In the stations of Manhattan
angels in syrupy soprano sing.
A fallen angel
snores in the subway train.

Miriam, schlage die Trommel:
"Quadriertes Frauenrecht!".
Simson, setz die Perücke auf
und zieh frisch ins Gefecht.
Josef, du gütiger Bankboß,
pfänd nicht unseren Kram.
Salomo, gib deinen Harem auf:
versuch's mal monogam.

Männlein und Weiblein Manhattans,
habt immer die Bibel parat,
in Leder mit Goldschnitt, in Technikolor
oder einfach im Taschenformat.

Miriam, beat the drum:
"Women's equal rights!"
Sampson, put your wig on
and go fresh into the fight.
Joseph, you good-natured bank boss,
don't impound our economy.
Salomon, give up your harem:
for once try monogamy.

Man and woman of Manhattan,
keep the Bible always nearby,
in leather, gilt-edged, Technicolor,
or simply pocket-sized.

MAX RODEN was born in Vienna in 1881. A theater and art critic, he was editor of the *Österreichische Volkszeitung*, published his first volume of poetry in 1906, and a translation of Robert Sherard's *The Life of Oscar Wilde* in 1908. He fled to New York in 1939, served at the war's end as a US correspondent for the *Wiener Zeitung*, and died in New York in 1968.

Erste Tage im Häusergebirge

Die Stadt erschien mir sehr bekannt.
Nicht schreckte mich Titanengier.
Sie schlang den weiten Arm um mich,
Und ihren Sang trug ich im Ohr.

Der Unschlaf macht in ihr sich breit.
Ich fiel in ihn und starrte groß.
Das Herz schlug den Maschinentakt.
Die Straßenschluchten dampften schwer.

Ich hing am Nervenstrang der Stadt.
Sie schrie in mich.
Ich schrie in sie.
Da schreckte sie mich sehr.

First Days in the Mountain Range of Houses

The city seemed quite familiar.
Titanic greed didn't frighten me.
It slung its wide arm around me,
And I carried its song in my ear.

Sleeplessness widens itself in it.
I fell into it, staring wide-eyed.
The heart beat the machines' rhythm.
The street-canyons steamed heavily.

I was tied to the nerves of the city.
It screamed into me.
I screamed into it.
It terrified me that way.

1940

Hirt ohne Herde

Zeichnet der Schritt seine Spuren?
Wirft einen Schatten das Ich?
Rühren die Zeiger der Uhren
träge im Zeitenkreis sich?

Bin ich noch Hirt einer Herde,
die sich in Worten ermißt?
Sprech ich, ein Schöpfer, das Werde,
das eines Gottes sonst ist?
Fragen verfolgen die Fragen.
Antworten stehn nicht bereit.
Unlust und Ungeduld ragen,
Türme der Qual, in die Zeit.

Düster ist alles Geschehen.
Hirt ohne Herde zu sein!
Fahnen der Einsamkeit wehen,
und es verstummen Schalmein.

Leb ich in Wäldern, auf Wiesen,
leb ich im Wirbel der Stadt,
überall hör ich nur diesen
Ton, der verfangen sich hat.

Der sich in lässige Ohren
drängt, ohne je zu vergehn.
Schritte und Ich sind verloren,
da die kein Ziel mehr ersehn.

Shepherd without a Flock

Does the footstep mark its own traces?
Is a shadow cast by the self?
Do the clocks' hands languidly circle
there, on the shelf?

Do I still shepherd a flock,
which expresses itself in words?
Do I speak, a creator, the "Let there be,"
which is a God's business?
Questions follow the questions.
Answers don't stand ready.
Listless impatience rises,
towers of torment, in time.

All events are dark.
To be a shepherd without a flock!
Flags of loneliness wave,
and pipes fall silently mute.

Living in woods, in meadows,
or in the city's vortex,
everywhere I hear only this
sound that's entangled itself.

It presses to casual ears
without ever fading away.
Footsteps and self are lost,
no longer seeing their goal.

Sekundenballade

Wie wenn du ertränkest, so ist es.
Das Leben, im Blitz, zieht vorüber.
Das Lichte wird lichter und trüber
das Trübe. Du bists nicht und bist es,
der still hält für reiche Sekunden,
an Traum und Erinnrung gebunden.

Was sollen die Strassen, die Gärten,
die Häuser, die rollenden Wagen?
Die Träume, die sie in dich tragen,
sind Weiser auf schwebenden Fährten.
An Traum und Erinnrung gebunden
durchlebst du die stillen Sekunden.

Blick auf! Über dir wölbt sich Bläue.
Blick um dich! Die Erde erblutet.
Der Blutstrom in dir überflutet
die Borde der Stille. Ins Neue
entreissen dich, stürmisch, Sekunden,
an Traum und Erinnrung gebunden.

Zu Purpur verdickt sich die Röte,
erstickend den Atem, umschnürt dir
die Kehle – stöhne! – und führt dir
heran schwere Bilder die Nöte.
Des Traums, der Erinnrung entbunden,
zersprühen die heissen Sekunden.

Die Taguhr ticktackt ihre Mahnung.
Du greifst an die Brust dir, und breiter
ergeht sich dein Atem und weiter
entfernen sich Mühung und Ahnung.
Es fallen hinab die Sekunden,
des Traums, der Erinnrung entbunden.

Ballad of the Seconds

Like when you drown, it's like that.
Life, in a flash, draws before you.
The light gets lighter, the dimness
dimmer. You are and aren't that,
which for rich seconds waits to see,
bound to dream and memory.

What are the streets, the gardens,
the houses, the rolling cars?
The dreams they inspire
are signposts on floating tracks.
Bound to dream and recollections
you live through quiet seconds.

Look up! Blueness arches above you.
Look around you! The earth is bleeding.
The bloodstream in you overfloods
the edges of silence. Into the new
you're town off by stormy seconds,
bound to dream and remembrance.

The redness thickens to purple,
stifling your breath, surrounds you
the throat – moan! – and leads to you
heavy pictures of hardships.
Released from the dream, from memory,
the hot seconds atomize, shimmering.

The calendar tick-tocks its reminder.
You touch your chest,
your breath deepening,
as effort, idea retreat further.
The seconds go on falling downward,
released from dream and remembrance.

Häuser meiner Heimat

Echowand der Schritte:
Häuser meiner Heimat.
Hab ich euch verlassen,
hallt mein Schreiten hohl.

Steht nicht überm Meere,
blau auf blau, der Himmel?
Aber meiner Heimat
Farbe ist es nicht.

Treibt nicht aus den Bergen
frohe Lust zum Tale?
Aber meiner Heimat
Atem ist es nicht.

Spürt ich dich nicht immer,
als ich in dir weilte,
spür ich dich, o Heimat,
bin ich nicht in dir.

Houses of my Homeland

Echo-wall of footsteps:
Houses of my homeland.
I've left you behind me,
my footsteps ring hollow.

Doesn't the sky stretch over the sea,
blue over blue?
But it isn't my
homeland's hue.

Doesn't glad joy
drive one from mountain to valley?
But it isn't my
homeland's breath.

I didn't always sense you,
while I was in you,
I feel you, oh homeland,
now that I'm not.

Fremde du, o Heimat du

Fremde du, o Heimat du,
nimm mich auf als deinen Sohn.
War ichs denn nicht immer schon,
ehe du mich kanntest?

Ist nicht alles vorbestimmt,
und man muss den Weg nur gehn?
Ohren hören, Augen sehn
doch nur das Bekannte.

Und die Sprache, die geheim
zugehört so Mensch wie Tier,
tönt sie nicht aus dir zu mir,
Fremde du, o Heimat?

Überall und nirgend ist
Heimat, eingeborne.
Der dem Sinn Verschworne
hat die Fremde nur.

Wenn sie ihm aus Sternen singt,
und das Lied sich in ihn senkt,
hört er, wie die Nacht sich denkt:
Menschlein in der Fremde.

You Foreign Land, oh You Homeland

You foreign land, you homeland,
take me as your son.
Wasn't I already one,
before you knew me?

Isn't all just predetermined,
so one can just follow the path?
Ears hear, eyes see
only what's known.

And what is language, which mysteriously
belongs to both man and beast,
doesn't it sound from you to me,
you foreign land, oh homeland?

Everywhere and nowhere is
homeland, the native sort.
Those to meaning sworn
have but the foreign land.

When it sings to him from stars,
and the song into him sinks,
he hears, as the night thinks:
little man in the foreign land.

In Wien 1956

Nun bin ich hier,
von wo ich ging,
als über mir
die schwarze Wolke hing.

Es rauschte schwer
in Baum und Strauch.
Von Dächern her
quoll dicker, rußiger Rauch.

Er deckte zu
so Mensch wie Haus.
Kein lichtes Du
erlöst sich daraus.

Die Zeit verging.
Die Zeit vergeht.
Sie schließt den Ring
um Trauer und Gebet.

Nein, nein, er engt
mich nicht mehr ein,
Befreit, beschenkt,
streif ich straßaus, gassein.

In Vienna 1956

Now here I am,
from whence I'd sprung,
as over me
the black cloud hung.

It rustled heavy
in tree and bush.
From rooftops
thick, sooty smoke pushed.

It swelled across
both man and house.
You let no light
escape its douse.

Time passed.
Time flies.
Closing the circle
round prayer and rites.

No, no, it hems
me in no more,
Set free, spared,
from street to alley I roam.

Sterben auch

Nacht, Ruhe, Schlaf.
Aus einer Quelle rieselt
das Wasser des Vergessens.
Der Leib ist in Kühle getaucht.
So ist das Sterben.

Zeichen ziehn
am Traumhimmel hin.
Lichte, leichte
Tauben im Fluge
weisen ins Weite.

Fern eine Rose
blättert sich auf.
Rosige Flocken
schweben hernieder.

Sieh, das Erwachen
versäumt sich nie.

Aber die Träume
sind Blüten im Schnee.
Und sie ersehnen
die strahlende Rose.

Sonne, o Rose du,
Himmelstraum seliger,
du auch versinkst
in der kühlenden Quelle,
schenkst dich, Erhabene,
schwankend im Abbild,
abendlich trauernd,

Death, too

Night, quiet, sleep.
From one spring trickles
the water of forgetting.
The flesh is submerged in coolness.
That's how dying is.

Signs move
across the dream sky.
Light, light
doves in flight
aim far away.

Distant, a rose
unfolds.
Rosy flakes
float down.

See, the awakening
never fails.

But dreams
are flowers in snow.
And they long for
the radiant rose.

Sun, oh you rose,
Heaven's dream blessed,
you, too sink
in the cooling spring,
give yourself, sublime,
swaying in image,
evening mourning,

der Quelle, dem Grab.
Ach, auch das Sterben
versäumt sich nie.

to the source, the grave.
Ah, death, too,
never fails.

MARGARETE KOLLISCH, born in Vienna in 1893, worked as a teacher, translator and journalist. In 1939, she and her husband, architect Otto Kollisch, and their two children immigrated to New York, where she worked for twenty-five years as a massage therapist while teaching German and French lessons, publishing in magazines and giving radio lectures. She was awarded a prize for foreign language poetry in 1969 by York College of City University of New York. She died in 1979 in New York.

New York Sky-Line

O Himmelslinie, unerreichbar einst
wie jenes Paradies, das du beweinst,
Vertriebener, von alter Angst gequält,
der nächtens ungeschlafne Stunden zählt,
bis dir erneut im blassen Morgenlicht
die Linie zeigt der Dächer Leichtgewicht,
so strebefest im Anschaun, Wand an Wand,
ein Hochgebirg, getürmt von Menschenhand,
mit Schroffen, Zacken, Zinnen, Vielgestalt
in Harmonie zum Einheitsbild geballt,
so tröstlich nah' und ahnungsvoll entfernt,
nicht weiß, nicht rot, nicht streifig, noch besternt,
nie familiar, doch namenlos vertraut,
des Himmels eingezeichnet keusche Braut, –
o Himmelslinie, kein Wort beschreibt,
was uns als Wort so innig einverleibt.

New York Skyline

Oh, skyline, unreachable once
like any paradise you mourn,
displaced person, tormented by old fears,
counting your sleepless hours at night,
until renewed by the dawn's early light
the skyline shows rooftops, so slight,
firmly joisted, wall to wall, in might,
high mountains towered with human hands,
with precipices, peaks, towers, multiform
in harmony and unity clenched,
so comfortingly close and ominously far,
not white, nor red, not streaked, nor starred,
never familiar, but namelessly well-known,
the sky's outlined chaste bride—
oh skyline, no word can describe
what in us as word is so profoundly inscribed.

Mai in der Wall Street

In der mittagsmüden Menge,
in dem Börsenmarktgedränge
sieht man nicht
unter künstlichen Fassaden,
übertüncht von Schönheitsläden
ein Gesicht.

Neu beschuht und neu gewandet,
alle Hälse schmuckumrandet,
aber kaum
unter Fähnchen oder Fahnen
regt sich ungewisses Ahnen,
blüht ein Traum.

Zwischen fremden Kapitalien
plagt sich jede mit Lappalien
wie sie kann,
wartet sehnlich auf den Freitag
auf den Zahltag, auf den Maitag,
auf ein bißchen FUN!

May in Wall Street

In the noon-weary bustle,
in the stock market's hustle
one doesn't see
under man-made façades,
beautician-whitewashed
a me.

Newly-shod and freshly-dressed,
all necks with jewels bedecked,
but hardly
under flags or banners
a vague inkling flatters
a blooming dream.

Between foreign capitals
they all plague themselves with trivia
as they can,
waiting eagerly for Friday
for payday, for May Day,
for a little FUN!

MIMI GROSSBERG

Sommernacht im Ft. Tryon Park

Riesenampel, rot,
hängt über'm Park der Mond.
Kein Stern am Himmel –
doch mildes Sodiumlicht
strömt auf vom Rasen
bis in die höchsten Wipfel alter Bäume.
Die Bühne ist bereit.
Wo bleibt Titania?
Steht Puck nicht hinter'm Strauch?
Und dort, auf jener Bank –
sieh: Hermia und Lysander!
Sie schläft . . . So hoffen wir,
dass Oberon ihr nicht
sein Zauberwasser auf die Augen spritzt
und sie sich nicht – erwachend –
für einen Esel erhitzt . . .

Midsummer Night in Fort Tryon Park

Great traffic light, red,
the moon hangs over the park.
Not a star in the heavens —
but mild sodium light
flows from the lawn
to the highest old treetops.
The stage is ready.
Where is Titania?
Doesn't Puck wait in the shrubs?
And there, on that park bench —
look: Hermia and Lysander!
She sleeps . . . Let's hope
Oberon's magic water
isn't o'er her sleeping eyes cast
so that she doesn't — awaking —
find herself hot for an ass . . .

OTTO FÜRTH, born in Strakonitz (today Strakonice, in the Czech Republic) in 1894, moved to Vienna at the age of four. Studying law when the First World War broke out, he enlisted as a soldier, was captured by the Russian army and shipped to a Siberian prisoner-of-war camp, but escaped to China, where he taught German and French. Back in Vienna at the war's end, he changed his studies to philosophy and German literature, completing a doctorate, publishing a collection of short stories, and writing well-received expressionist plays. Fürth was traveling in Switzerland for theater work when the Second World War broke out, and was able to leave with his wife and children for New York in 1941. He worked in a department store warehouse until finding a job as an accountant with the Wall Street firm Lazard. The author of an autobiographical novel *Flucht aus dem Schicksal* (*Flight from Fate*) and the novel *Men in Black* ("written," Fürth himself wrote, "for a political [anti-Nazi] purpose"), he died in New York in 1979.

Lied des kleinen Angestellten

Ich bin ein kleiner Angestellter
In einem großen Warenhaus.
Ich werde alle Tage älter
Und trotz Erhöhung der Gehälter
Komm ich mit meinem Lohn nicht aus.

In diesem Land von Milch und Honig
Trink ich synthetischen Kaffee.
In fernsehfreudiger Platonik
Betrachte ich „per Electronic"
Was ich im Leben niemals seh'.

Sooft es dämmert oder nachtet,
Werd' ich als menschliches Paket
Mit tausend andern, unbeachtet,
In einen dunklen Zug verfrachtet,
Der durch die Untergründe geht.

Doch oberirdisch in den Staaten
Erfreu' ich mich der Hochkultur
Mit hundertfältigen Apparaten.
Und alles kaufe ich auf Raten,
Vom Eigenheim zur Taschenuhr.

Nur in den Nächten, klar und kälter,
Schau ich verstört nach Sternen aus.
. . . Ich werde alle Jahre älter . . .
Ich bin ein kleiner Angestellter
In einem großen Warenhaus.

Song of the Minor Employee

I'm a minor employee
In a big department store.
Growing older each day
Despite rises in pay
I can't manage my bills anymore.

In this land of milk and honey
I drink synthetic coffee.
In joyful television Platonics
I look "through electronics"
At what I'll never in my life see.

Whenever it dawns or grows dark,
I'm like a human package
With a thousand others, unremarked,
Shipped in a dark train,
That runs through the subways.

While aboveground in the States
I enjoy high culture
With hundreds of apparatuses.
And buy everything on installment,
To watch from my house.

Only nights, clear and colder,
I look up, distracted, toward stars.
. . . Every year I grow older . . .
I'm a minor employee
In a big department store.

Wall Street, 47. Stock

Zuweilen fällst du aus der Welt,
Wie nachts ein Kind aus seinem Bette fällt,
Auf kühlen harten Grund hinaus;
Es späht empor, scheu, mit gekreuzten Beinen,
Zu Pölstern, die wie ferne Berge scheinen,
Und alles sieht so fremd und seltsam aus.

. . . Du wanderst zwischen breiten Häusertürmen,
Auf glatten Gassen, die von Wagen wimmeln.
Und Untergrund und Hochbahnviadukt
Erdonnern dumpf, geschüttelt wie von Stürmen,
Und ihre bunten Menschenfrachten warden
Von tausend Türen gierig eingeschluckt.
Die kleine russgeschwärzte Kirche läutet
Neunfach den Werktag ein,
Und hunderttausend Pulte werden aufgesperrt.

Du bist mir dieser Alltagswelt vertraut,
Dein grünes Löschpapier ist deine Wiese,
Elektrisch überweht von einer Brise.
In schwarzen Muscheln, die an Drähten hängen,
Sind ferne körperlose Stimmen laut.
Die Ziffern schwirren, die Sekunden drängen.

. . . Und plötzlich, mitten in der Wichtigkeit
Von einem Handel, einer Transaktion –
Traf dich ein Sonnenblitz? Ein Vogelton?
Ein Hauch, der von verhüllten Dingen kündet? –
Auf einmal fällst du aus dem Gang der Zeit,
Aus all den engen Grenzen deiner Welt,
So wie ein Kind des Nachts aus seinem Bette fällt.
Du trittst ans Fenster, blickst zum Strom hinaus,

Wall Street, 47th Floor

Sometimes you fall out of the world,
Like a child falls from bed at night,
On cool hard ground you range;
Peeking up, shy, with crossed legs,
To pillows like distant mountains,
And everything looks so strange.

. . .You wander between wide house towers,
On slippery streets teeming with cars.
And subway and elevated train viaduct
Begin to thunder dully, shaken as from storms,
And its colorful human cargos are
Swallowed by a thousand greedy doors.
The little soot-blackened church rings
The working day nine times in,
And a hundred thousand desks are opened.

You are familiar with this everyday world,
Your green blotting paper is your meadow,
Electrically blown by a breeze.
In black shells hanging from wires,
Are distant disembodied voices loud.
The numbers buzz, the seconds press.

. . . And suddenly, in the middle of the importance
Of a trade, a transaction —
Did a sunburst hit you? A bird song?
A breath that tells of veiled things? —
Suddenly you fall out of the flow of time,
Out of all the narrow limits of your world,
Like a child falling out of bed at night.
You step to the window, watch the stream outside,

Der unten tief im breiten Hafen mündet:
Und Schiffe, Häuser, Wagen, kleine Menschen,
Das alles sieht wie fremdes Spielzeug aus.

That far below opens on the harbor wide:
And ships, houses, cars, tiny people,
All look like strange toys.

ROSE AUSLÄNDER was born in 1901 in Czernowitz (Chernivtsi) into a German-speaking family which fled to Vienna during the First World War as Russian troops invaded. While settled temporarily in Vienna, she began to write. Ausländer moved to Minneapolis in 1921, then to New York, where she worked as a journalist, taking US citizenship in 1926. She returned to Czernowitz in 1931 to care for her mother, thus losing her US citizenship, while teaching English, editing a newspaper, and completing her New York Cycle poems (many now lost). As she was Jewish, her first volume of poetry was banned in Germany and, being written in German, her work was banned from publication in Romanian journals. Her book's print run, never distributed, was destroyed by Nazis when Germany invaded Ukraine. Sent to a forced labor camp and listed for deportation, she hid in friends' basements until the city was annexed by the Soviet Union in 1944. Forbidden to carry her manuscripts with her, she copied as many as she could into tiny notebooks, smuggling them out on one of the last transports to leave the city, and fled to New York, reinstating her US citizenship. She died in Düsseldorf in 1988. A close friend of Paul Celan, whom she met while in hiding, she published seven volumes of poetry, writing only in English from 1948-1956.

Biographische Notiz

Ich rede
von der brennenden Nacht
die gelöscht hat
der Pruth

von Trauerweiden
Blutbuchen
verstummtem Nachtigallengesang

vom gelben Stern
auf dem wir
stündlich starben
in der Galgenzeit

nicht über Rosen
red ich

Fliegend
auf einer Luftschaukel
Europa Amerika Europa

ich wohne nicht
ich lebe

Biographical Note

I speak
of the burning night
quenched by
the Prut[1]

of weeping willows
beeches
nightingale song fallen silent

of the yellow star
on which we
died by the hour
in the gallows-time

not about roses
speak I

Flying
on an air-swing
Europe America Europe

I don't reside[2]
I live

---

1   River forming the borders of Ukraine, Moldavia and Romania, till 1939 partly
within the Republic of Poland. A more famous poem describing the region is
Sydir Vorobkevych's "Within that Prut Valley" (Над Прутом у лузі), translated
by Waldimir Semenyna (13 October 1933, *Ukrainian Weekly*), which includes the
lines: "Within that Prut Valley a cabin rests close / In which lives a lassie — a
beautiful rose: / Her eyes like the bright stars that lighten the sky; / When you
see them, laddie, you'll pause with a sigh. [...] Within that Prut Valley the flowers
are plucked / And wreathes for the wedding with myrtle are tucked; / Inside of
the cabin play fiddles and bass / While friends sing together: To their Happiness!"
2   The German word "wohnen" has roots in "Weide"—in Middle High Ger-
man: "to be happy," but originally: "to stay in a cherished space."

Harlem bei Nacht

Er zieht lange Fäden
aus der Trompete
wickelt sie
um Harlems
Dickicht.

Aus seinen Afrikaaugen
rollen weiche Streifen
Schwermut.

Raketenpilze
schießen in den
Negerhimmel
zerstäuben
über dem Blues.

Nur das Echo
taumelt noch ein paar Meilen
eh es die Seele
aushaucht.

Harlem by Night

He draws long threads
from the trumpet
wraps them
around Harlem's
thicket.

From his African eyes
roll soft streaks
of melancholy.

Rocket mushrooms
shoot in the
black man's heavens
atomize
above the blues.

Only the echo
staggers a few more miles
before it
breathes its last breath.

Chinatown

Enge Gäßchen
quer und quer
senfgewürzt.
Lotrechte Namen
über Buddhas und Tand.

Im Keller
das Halbdunkle duftet nach
Lampions und Limonen
über Papierbrücken.
Musik der Stäbchen
auf Porzellan
wo rosa der Hummer ruht zwischen
Stengeln und Saft.

Pfauen öffnen blaue Fächer
auf Seidenärmel.
Die kleine Frau im Kimono
beschwört den Teegeist
in der Kanne.

6000 Jahre
in schwarze Augen geschlitzt
das Erbe verbergend.

Um das verschwiegene Viertel
sieh die Chinesische Mauer
himmelhoch gezogen von
dünnen Pinseln und
Konfuziuslehren.

Chinatown

Narrow alleys
cross and cross
mustard-spiced.
Vertical names
over Buddhas and trinkets.

In the basement
the half-light is scented with
lanterns and lemons
over paper bridges.
Music of chopsticks
on porcelain
where, pink, the lobster rests between
stems and juice.

Peacocks open blue fans
on silk sleeves.
The little woman in a kimono
summons the tea spirit
in the pot.

6000 years
slotted in black eyes
hiding the heritage.

Round the secretive neighborhood
see the Great Wall
pulled sky-high by
thin brushes and
Confucian teachings.

Park Avenue Party

Während Januar die Gassen pudert, Bogenlampen den
Abend in Zitronenranken verzaubern, Gummireifen das
Pflaster schleifen in gleichmäßigen rotgrünen Abständen,
konzentriert sich der Samstagabend auf eine Wohnung
in der Park Avenue.

Fünfzig Freunde und Feinde werden traktiert mit Wangen-
küssen und geölter Herzlichkeit. Die erste Phase der
Verwirrung spült ein Cocktail herunter.

Gruppen um Leckerbissen, Whisky, Likör. Die Menschen-
liebe erstreckt sich vom Bartisch bis ins verwandelte
Gastzimmer. Der Speisetisch biegt sich von Fleisch,
Fisch, Gelee, Salat, Pralinen, Früchten, Nüssen, Kuchen,
Kaffee. Witze schlagen Wurzeln am Sofa, das aus allen
Polstern lacht.

Die Menschenliebe wird andauernd umgruppiert, das
Ritual des Lächelns läuft von Gesicht zu Gesicht,
Kerzen färben die Stimmung rot, Nischen sind ein
flüsternder Sommer, den keine Icecream abkühlt.

Aus dem Wein fliegen Lieder, Tanzrhythmen aus den
Rillen. Die Menschenliebe gruppiert sich um und um
nach Alter, Geschlecht, Reichtum und Rang,

während Schnee die Gassen verzaubert und die Stern-
augen der Nacht die Uhren hypnotisieren.

Park Avenue Party

As January dusts the alleys, streetlights enchant the
evening in lemon lines, car tires
grind patches at even red-green intervals,
Saturday night focuses on an apartment
in Park Avenue.

Fifty friends and enemies are tormented with cheek-
kisses and oiled cordiality. The first phase of the
confusion is flushed down with a cocktail.
Groups round delicacies, whiskey, liqueur.

Camaraderie extends from the bar table to the repurposed
bedroom. The dining table bends with meat,
fish, aspic, salad, chocolates, fruits, nuts, cake,
coffee. Jokes take root on the sofa, which laughs
from every cushion.

The camaraderie is constantly regrouped, the
ritual of the smile runs from face to face,
candles color the mood red, niches are a
whispering summer that no ice cream cools.

Songs fly from the wine, dance rhythms from the
record grooves. The camaraderie groups and regroups, this way and that
by age, sex, wealth and rank,

while snow enchants the streets and the star-
eyes of the night hypnotize the wristwatches.[1]

---

1 "That all was not well amongst [early postwar] Austrian émigré circles was
clear for any reader to see, and the literary émigrés themselves contributed
to this picture of internal divisions and rivalries" (Bushell 203).

Mit giftblauem Feuer

Sie kamen mit giftblauem Feuer
versengten unsere Kleider und Haut.

Der Blitz ihres Lachens schlug an unsre Schläfe
unsere Anwort war der Donner Jehovas.

Wir stiegen in den Keller, er roch nach Gruft.
Treue Ratten tanzten mit unsern Nerven.

Sie kamen mit giftblauem Feuer unser Blut zu verbrennen.
Wir waren die Scheiterhaufen unsrer Zeit.

With poison-blue fire

They came with poison-blue fire
scorched our clothes and skin.

The lightning of their laughter hit our temple
our answer was Jehovah's thunder.

We climbed to the cellar, it smelled of tomb.
Faithful rats danced with our nerves.

They came with poison-blue fire to burn our blood.
We were the funeral pyres of our age.

HERMANN BROCH, born in 1886 in Lower Austria, became internationally-known for his modernist trilogy *The Sleepwalkers* (1930/1932). In 1938 he was arrested, but managed to flee, leaving everything he owned in Austria and boarding a plane to London. With the help of James Joyce, Thomas Mann, and Albert Einstein, he secured a US visa, and quickly applied for citizenship. Entranced with 1930s New York, he also found America beset with the potential hazards of European-style fascism, and regretted being unable to join the US military to fight Hitler in Europe. As the Cold War began, he suggested that both western capitalism and Soviet communism showed dangerous signs of moving toward totalitarianism. He was a professor at Yale and Princeton, co-founded the Aurora Press, was nominated for a Nobel Prize in 1950, and died in New Haven in 1951.

Dank für ein leeres Blatt

Ein leeres Blatt von einer lieben Hand,
und zwischen ungeschriebnen Worten, ungeschriebnen Zeilen,
wo Sprache und Gedicht sich im Gedanken teilen,
in diesen Zwischenraum ist viel gebannt:

ein Zwischenraum von einem Punkt und trotzdem vielen Meilen,
in dem nichts steht und alles stand,
im Pausenzeichen Lied, da hab ich dich erkannt,
und nur der Zwischenraum ist das Verweilen.

Oh dunkler Zwischenraum des Seins, in dem wir leben
in einer Spannung zwischen Nichts und Nichts,
hier mag's uns glücken, einen Traum zu heben,
vom Herz gesät und vom Verstand gemäht,
und dem Geschöpf im Zwischen-Raum des Lichts
vom Lichte hergeweht
— du stummes Lied —
wird Leere zum Gebet.

Für T.L. 1942

Thanks for a Blank Page

A blank page from a dear hand got,
and between unwritten words, unwritten lines,
where language and poetry divide in thought,
from this in-between space much is left excised:

an in-between space of a single point, yet many miles,
in which nothing stands, yet all stood,
in the interlude, there I recognized you,
and only in the in-between space one rests a while.

Oh dark in-between space of being, in which we live
in a tension between nothing and nothing,
here perhaps we can manage to raise a dream,
sown from the heart, and by the mind reaped,
and for the creature in the in-between space of light
from the light blown there
— you mute song —
emptiness becomes prayer.

For T.L.   1942

Für ein Gästebuch

Jeder wandert, jeder weiß es,
doch es hält ihn auf den Straßen,
bis ihn durch die Nebelmassen
scheu ein Licht blinkt wie ein leises
Hoffen und wie Zielerfassen,
wie ein Ahnen jenes Preises,
der als Schluß des Wanderkreises
Rückkunft heißt im Ruhenlassen:
namenloser Gast ist jeder,
bis den Namen er darf schreiben,
nur ein Wort, ein Zug der Feder,
dennoch Zeichen für ein Bleiben,
selbstsichfindend, Ruh im Wandern
bei dem Freund, das Ich im andern.

Für Henry und Marion Seidel-Canby 1939

For a Guestbook

Everyone wanders, everyone knows it,
so it keeps him on the streets,
till through the thick fog it peeps
a shy light blinks like a quiet
hope and like a target,
like a sensing of that prize,
that as the close of the wanderer's route
means returning to rest:
each is a nameless guest,
till he can write his name,
just a word, a stroke of the quill,
yet a signal one might stay,
finding oneself, peace on the trek
with the friend, the "I" in the other.

For Henry und Marion Seidel-Canby 1939

Tu dein Leben nicht vertandeln
in dem tiefverschlafnen Wandeln,
wie es dieser Autor tat;
laß dein Leben nicht versklaven
von dem wandelbaren Schlafen:
jeder kriegt sein Eigentliches,
doch verliert's in seiner Nacht —
frage nicht: warum entwich es?

Für H.L.
    mit den "Schlafwandlern"

Don't spoil your life
in sleepwalking,
as this author did;
don't let your life be enslaved
by rote sleep:
each gets his own,
but loses it in his night —
don't ask: why did it escape?

> *For H.L.*
> with *The Sleepwalkers*[1]

---

1 The title of Broch's novels trilogy, and more recently of *The Sleepwalkers: How Europe Went to War in 1914* by historian Christopher Clark.

Zum Beispiel: Walt Whitman

Wo die Halme sprießen, in des Seins irdischer Mitte,
dort hebt die Dichtung an:
doch sie reicht bis zu des Lebens äußerster Grenze,
und siehe, die ist nicht außen,
die ist in der Seele.
Innen die Grenze und außen die Mitte,
eines das andere gebärend, eines dem andern verwoben,
das allein ist Dichtung —
Freilich, am Ende entdeckst du verwundert,
daß es einfach dein Leben,
das Leben des Menschen ist.

Für H.L.
mit den "Leaves of Grass"
1943

For Example: Walt Whitman

Where the stalks sprout, in the earthly center of being,[1]
there grows poetry:
but it reaches to life's outermost border,
and look, that border is not on the outside,
but in the soul.
Inside is the border and outside the center,
each bears the other, one entwines the other,
that's all poetry is —
Of course, in the end, bewildered, you discover,
that it's simply your life,
the life of mankind.

For H.L.
with "Leaves of Grass"
1943

---

1   Whitman's volume uses the word "stalk" to describe dead, gathered, or dried stalks, or as a verb, "stalking," frequently with ominous overtones: "stalks [...] brandishing the dagger in her hand." *Halme* can be either wheat or grass, and Whitman uses "grass" variously to describe lawns, grave-coverings, and prairie hay, with either simple or luxuriant connotations.

FRIEDRICH BERGAMMER, born in Vienna in 1909, followed his father in a career as an art expert and dealer, publishing his first book of short stories at the age of seventeen, and co-founding the literary journal *Das Silberboot*. After being briefly imprisoned in 1938, he fled to New York, working in his father's art dealership, and taking it over in 1952, while publishing volumes of his poetry in Austria after the war. He died in New York in 1981.

Kurzer Monolog in der Fremde

Verliere nicht dein Herz an die Vollendung!
Die Fremdsprache, in täglicher Verwendung
erübt, klingt reiner und wirkt plötzlich flach . . .

Er dachte nach. Ach, der Akzent wird zu schwach.
Einst war er stark. Er schwindet. Es vergeht
ein falscher Ton, der Früheres verrät.

Trug er, ein kräftiger Christophorus,
das Kind aus seiner Heimat durch den Fluß?

Short Monologue in a Foreign Land

Don't lose your heart in the aim of perfection!
Foreign language, with daily correction
tones cleaner, sounding suddenly pat . . .

He thought on that. Oh, the accent's gone flat.
First it was strong. Now it wanes,
that false tone, which used to give you away.
Did he carry, a strong Saint Christopher,
the child from his homeland across the river?

FRITZ BRAININ

E.A. Poe-Park Terrace

Die ich am liebsten hab',
wohnt rückwärts im Parterre,
wo ich mich gern vergrab',
als ob in Wien ich wär.

Am Abend, wenn durchs rosa
Licht ich 'runter lauf',
kehrt sich die Welt der Prosa
um in ein Gedicht.

Sie grüßt mich, heiß vom Kochen
einer Kleinigkeit . . .
Am Ende einer Wochen
hat man wieder Zeit.

Mit ihrem Kellerfenster
(wo man nichts sollte sehn
als gehsteig-hoch Gespenster?)
ein Wunder ist geschehn:

Tief unten die Terrasse
braust im Sodiumlicht!
O Venus, wolkennasse,
schwindelnd komm in Sicht!

Und wenn uns welt-versäumend
das Tonband Weills Jazz bringt,
dann schreib' ich, während sie träumend
und tellerwaschend singt.

Poe Park Terrace[1]

She whom I like best
lives in back on the ground floor,
where I happily bury myself,
as if in Vienna once more.

In the evening, when through pink
light I "head downstairs,"
the world of prose turns
into a poem.

She greets me, hot from cooking
some little thing . . .
At the end of a week
one finds time again.

With her basement window
(where one shouldn't see
anything but sidewalk-high ghosts?)
a miracle has happened:

Far below, the terrace
buzzes in sodium light!
Oh cloud-damp Venus,
come dizzily in sight!

And as, world-lost,
the tape player brings us Weill's jazz,[2]
then I write, while she, dreaming
and doing the dishes, sings.

1   Also published (in slightly different form) as "1949: Upper-Manhattan
Lieder (An eine Gertrude Steinsche Exilantenmuse)."
2   Kurt Weill.

Das siebte Wien
(Jamaica, Queens)

Ein Mädel rieb ihr Fenster rein
beim elektrischen Hochbahngleis.
Ein Greis sitzend still im Abendschein.
O, Kind schwarz mit Katze weiß!

Sanft leuchtete der Himmel wie Zinn,
spät ein Durch-Zug schnurrte fern . . .
Und wenn ich auch begriff den Sinn
des Lebens auf diesem Stern,

war ich einsamer noch als Monds Immigranten:
Jeder Vers, den ich schrieb, schien dumm,
wo parallel Geleise brannten
zum Reim im Infinitum.

The Seventh Vienna[1]
(Jamaica, Queens)

A girl wiped her window clean
by the electric elevated train rail.
An old man sitting still in the evening's gleam.
Oh, black child with white cat!

Gently the sky shone like tin,
a late through-train purred in the distance far . . .
And even if I understood the sense
of life on this star,

then I would be lonelier still than moon immigrants:
Each verse I wrote seemed silly,
where parallel tracks burnt
to rhyme in infinity.

---

1 Possibly a reference to Anna Seghers's *The Seventh Cross* (1942), whose plot
centers on escaped concentration camp prisoners.

42nd Street Library

Der Bibliotheksgong jagt mich fort
aus meinem Leserparadies!
Nie parkt am Sessel nachts mein Hemd.
Nie seh ich Mondlicht auf dem Fries.

Bei Tag mein Heimweh ich verlier,
wenn ich besuch das Steinlöwenhaus,
wo ich mit Dichtern kopulier . . .
In Büchern nur kenn ich mich aus.

Wie Ginseng-Tee packst du mir ein
Franz Kafkas Amerika nach mittags . . .
Im Geist bin ich nicht mehr allein,
Café-Genossen Wiens und Prags!

Bis ich einmal (wie überschwemmt
von Kramers Einsamkeit!) noch bleib,
dann parkt am Sessel nachts mein Hemd,
wirst du, Bibliothek, mein Weib.

42nd Street Library[1]

The library's closing bell chases me
from my reader's paradise!
Never park my shirt on the armchair, nights.
Never see moonlight on the frieze.

By day I lose my homesickness,
when I visit the stone lions' house,
where I copulate with poets . . .
Only in books do I know my way around.

Like ginseng tea you pack me up
Franz Kafka's Amerika after noon . . .
In spirit I'm no longer alone,
Café-comrades of Vienna and Prague!

Until I once (as if overwhelmed
with Kramer's loneliness!) still remain,[2]
then my shirt is parked on the armchair, nights,
you become, library, my wife.

---

1 One of several poems written in New York with the heading "Englisch-Klas-
senübungen" (English class work).
2 Theodore Kramer, Austrian poet exiled to Great Britain during the Second
World War.

FRANZ CARL WEISKOPF was born in 1900 in Prague to a bilingual family. Though a student of German literature, he rejected the rising German nationalism in Czechoslovakia after the First World War. He published under various pseudonyms before moving to Berlin to edit the newspaper *Berlin am Morgen*. When Nazis took control of the German government in 1933, he returned to Prague to edit the newspaper *Arbeiter-Illustrierte-Zeitung*. When Germany invaded Czechoslovakia in 1938, the newspaper was closed down and Weiskopf fled to Paris. Hitler invaded Poland while Weiskopf was on a speaking tour of the United States organized by the League of American Writers, so he and his wife remained in New York until 1949. Afterward, he worked at the Czechoslovakian embassy in Washington, then served as Czechoslovakian ambassador to Sweden and China, before moving to East Berlin in 1953, where he co-edited a literary journal, publishing his own novels, short stories, essays and poetry, before dying in 1955. He is best remembered as a master of short prose anecdotes.

A Library in New York
(Eine Bibliothek in New York)
1945

At the head of Second Avenue, right near St. Mark's Place, where scents of Italian spaghetti, Ukrainian borsch, Polish sausage and Yiddish "Gefilte Fish" happily mingle, sits a branch of the New York Public Library. This branch carries a German name—that of German-Moravian Oswald Ottendorfer, who has a very honorable place in the history of New York's journalism and public libraries.[1]

Beautiful old colonial-style furniture sits on the library's upper floor for one to sink into. One feels and soon is at home. From the shelves on the walls, one is greeted by many, many familiar names: Goethe, Heine, Lessing, Herder, Schiller, Hölderlin, Büchner, the Mann brothers, Werfel, Feuchtwanger, next to them also the kitschy and mendacious bards from Karl May to Eschtrut and Zillich. But more or less predominating are the good names, and anti-Nazi German literature is very well-represented . . . much better than in most public libraries back home. In particular, the new acquisitions of the last eight to ten years show how much good will, taste and sincere love for free German literature has been and is at work here. Charlotte Hubach, the librarian, and her staff are thus more than just employees of an American library with substantial German-language book holdings.[2] They understand how to encourage a friendly, living relationship with many German-language writers from Germany, Austria, and Czechoslovakia. The library's beautiful reading room has served among other things as a worthy showplace and setting for a great evening of Slav poetry in German translation.

The portrait of Oswald Ottendorfer—as we find him in the New York newspaper offices of the *Deutsche Staatszeitung*—

shows a sturdily-built man with a powerful head, whose wide bearded chin rests above a necktie, between the two white wings of a high collar from 1870 or 1880. Ottendorfer's biography must be picked out from various brochures and from the *Sudetendeutsche Lebensbilder* which Professor Gierach, who became ingloriously known as a prophet of Konrad Henlein, has laid out.[3] (How would it have been, if one of our anti-Nazi historians and biographers had produced an Ottendorfer biography?) After sorting through diverse nationalistic fancy dressings, one comes across a picture in which he much resembles Hans Kudlich.[4] Like Kudlich, Ottendorfer (a cloth-maker's son from Zwittau) was a student in Vienna and took part in the revolutionary fight of '48 as a member of the Academic Legion.[5] He was member of the defenders of Vienna's Rasumofskybrücke against the Croatian battalions of the Habsburg reaction to the uprisings and protests. Like Kudlich, Ottendofer, too had to flee after the revolution's defeat and was sentenced to death in absentia by a Habsburg court. Like Kudlich, he went to America, where he found a second homeland. As editor, then editor-in-chief of the New York *Deutsche Staatszeitung*,[6] Ottendorfer lead an incessant fight against backwardness, corruption, and obscurantism. The first defeat of the infamous Tammany Hall, which had controlled New York, is to be laid on Ottendorfer's account.

A true democrat, he refused to participate in any form of racism. Above all, he commended the German-American press to serve truth and freedom.

He provided his hometown Zwittau with funds to build a public library—the first of its kind in Central Europe.

He also gifted a library to his second hometown, New York. He died in December 1900. In one of his last public speeches he warned German-Americans: "Never forget, you should be working in the service of humanity."

---

1 New York's first free public library, opened in 1883.

2 In 1939 Hubach was optimistic that American libraries were centers of enculturation for refugees from Europe, providing "a wonderful opportunity here as librarians to sell America and the idea of a democratic state to these bewildered people."
3 Erich Gierach, the best-known Nazi-allied German literature scholar of the 1930s.
4 Nineteenth-century Austrian/Czech parliamentarian who pushed for an end to forced peasant labor in 1848, fled to Germany and Switzerland in 1849 when the uprisings were crushed, then to Hoboken, New Jersey, helping found the Hoboken Academy in 1861.
5 A military organization of some 6,000 Viennese students organized in 1848, in large part to end censorship, topple the Metternich administration and form a new constitution.
6 Founded in the 1830s, and to date the longest continuously-running newspaper in the United States, in any language.

FRIEDRICH BERGAMMER

Rot-Weiß-Rot

„Das Schönste an der amerikanischen Flagge
sind ihre rot-weiß-roten Streifen",
sagte ein österreichischer Einwanderer
nach siebenunddreißig Jahren
und meinte es nicht wegwerfend –
Amerika wegwerfend –, sondern im Gegenteil
dankbar, daß dieser große Kontinent
langsam die Farbe seiner Heimat annahm.

Red-White-Red

"The most beautiful part of the American flag
is its red-white-red stripes,"
said an Austrian immigrant
after thirty-seven years
and didn't mean it disdainfully –
America disdaining —, but on the contrary
thankful, that this great continent
had slowly taken on the colors of his homeland.

GRETA HARTWIG-MANSCHINGER was born in Vienna in 1899. A writer of radio shows and cabaret texts, she fled to France in 1938, then to the United States in 1940. An actress, she wrote opera librettos for her husband Kurt Manschinger (Ashley Vernon), and published the social realist novel *Rendezvous in Manhattan*. She died in Florida in 1971.

Ein Mann hat Heimweh

Die Heimat verloren, die Träume zerronnen;
ich hab' es getragen, ich glaub', wie ein Mann.
Ich habe mein Leben von vorne begonnen,
New York ist der Schmelztiegel, wo man es kann.
Wenn ich Heimweh hab', bild' ich mir ein,
dass mein Coca-Cola ein Glas Wein,
dass der Woolworth der Herzmansky ist
und im Hudsontal die Donau fliesst.
Ist der "Hector" nicht ein Ringcafé?
und die Eastside Franz-Josefs Kai?
Und der Times Square ist der Stefansplatz
und das Drugstore Counter-Girl mein Schatz;
für Grand Central setz' ich Westbahn hin,
für die Liberty – die "Spinnerin";
und der Bronxer Zoo ist mein Schönbrunn,
wo der Aff' sich kratzt am After-noon.
Wenn ich Heimweh hab', bild' ich mir's ein
und dann fühl ich mich nicht so allein.

Ich sparte und legte das Geld schön beiseite
und endlich, da fuhr ich auf Urlaub nach Wien.
Doch alles war anders, die Stadt und die Leute,
's war seltsam! New York ging mir nicht aus dem Sinn.
Ich hab' Heimweh! Und so will ich mein
g'wohntes Coca-Cola, keinen Wein;
einen Woolworth, wo Herzmansky ist,
einen Hudson, wo die Donau fliesst,
einen "Hector", nicht ein Ringcafé
und die East Side statt dem Franz-Josefs Kai;
einen Times Square, keinen Stefansplatz
und ein Drugstore Counter-Girl als Schatz.
Westbahnhof? Da g'hört Grand Central hin!

A Man is Homesick

The homeland lost, the dreams depart;
I've born it, I think, like a man.
I've begun my life again from the start,
New York's the melting pot where you can.
    When I'm homesick, I imagine I find
    my Coca-Cola's a glass of wine,
    that Woolworth's aisles are Herzmansky's window shows[1]
    and in the Hudson valley the Danube flows.
    Isn't Hector's diner a Ring café?[2]
    and the East Side, Franz-Josef Kai?
    And Times Square's the Stefansplatz
    and the drug store counter girl my *Schatz*;
    at Grand Central Station, I'd put the Westbahn in,
    for the Statue of Liberty – the "Spinnerin,"[3]
    and the Bronx Zoo is my Schönbrunn,
    where the ape scratches its backside all afternoon.[4]
    When I'm homesick, I imagine it so
    and then I don't feel quite so alone.

I saved and saved, laying money aside
and finally, went to Vienna on vacation.
But everything was different, the city, peoples' stride,
it was strange! New York ran through my thoughts in rotation.
    I'm homesick! And so I want mine
    to be a Coca-Cola, not wine;
    a Woolworth's, where Herzmansky stands,
    a Hudson, where the Danube wends,
    a Hector's, not a Ring café,
    and the East Side, not Franz-Josef Kai;
    a Times Square, instead of Stefansplatz
    and a drug store counter girl as my *Schatz*.
    Westbahnhof? That's where Grand Central should have
    been!

LIBERTY anstatt der "Spinnerin"!
Einen Bronxer Zoo anstatt Schönbrunn,
wo sich jeder kratzt am After-noon!
Ich kann diesen Wandel nicht verstehn.
Wien, ach warum ließest du mich gehn!

Lady Liberty instead of the "Spinnerin!"
    A Bronx Zoo instead of Schönbrunn,
    where they scratch their bums, afternoons!
    I cannot understand this change. Oh —
    Vienna, why'd you let me go!

---

1 A famous Viennese department store, opened in 1863, "Aryanized" in 1938, and returned to its owners in 1948.
2 A diner in New York's meat-packing district, opened in 1949.
3 Viennese monument erected in 1375, supposedly where the wife of a crusader sat waiting, spinning, for his return from war.
4 "After" in German is slang for "backside" (buttocks).

THEODOR KRAMER, born in 1897 in Lower Austria, moved to Vienna in 1908. He was badly wounded in the First World War. By 1931 he was a self-supporting author, and a member of the United Socialist Writers. Thomas Mann called him one of the greatest poets of his generation, and his works include over 10,000 poems, some of which have been set to music. In 1939 he fled to England, and was interned in Liverpool, then on the Isle of Man. From 1943-1957 he worked as a librarian in Guilford, Surrey. In 1957 he returned to Vienna, where he died in 1958, without funds and largely forgotten, following a brain hemorrhage. In 1984 the Theodor Kramer Gesellschaft was founded in Vienna to research his work and to promote refugee and resistance literature through contacts with refugee writers and artists.

Wiedersehen mit der Heimat

Nach Jahren kam, verstört,
ich wieder her;
der alten Gassen manche
sind nicht mehr,
der Ringturm kantig
sich zum Himmel stemmt:
Erst in der Heimat bin ich ewig fremd.

Mir schließt sich im Gedächtnis
nicht das Loch;
Espresso glitzern,
mich empfängt kein Tschoch,
das Moped braust,
nur hastig wird geschlemmt:
Erst in der Heimat bin ich ewig fremd.

Sind auch die Lüfte anderswo bewohnt,
mir ist, als zielte alles
nach dem Mond,
der saugte,
zwischen Dächern eingeklemmt:
Erst in der Heimat bin ich ewig fremd.

Reunion with the Homeland

Years later I came back, distraught,
me, back here once more;
some of the old streets
are no more,
the Ringturm, ranges[1]
toward heaven, angular:
Only in the homeland am I forever a stranger.

In my memory, the gap
stays unfilled;
glittering espresso,
no toil awaits me,
the moped roars,
people feast hastily:
Only in the homeland am I forever a stranger.

Though the skies are also inhabited elsewhere,
it comes to me, as if everything aimed
to the moon,
which suckles,
pinched between rooftops' ranges:
Only in the homeland am I forever a stranger.[2]

---

1 A Viennese skyscraper completed in 1955, built on the only lot on the
Schottenring that was completely bombed out during the Second World War.
2 One of Kramer's last poems.

ALFRED SCHICK was born in Vienna in 1897. A doctor, clinical psychiatrist, and author of poems and essays, and fled Austria for New York in 1938. He died during a holiday in Salzburg in 1977.

Wieder in Wien

Ich wander strassentlang betäubt umher.
Die Strassen blicken tot und leer.
Die Jahre sind mir schon verblichen,
Die Jugend ist mir längst entwichen.

Da steigen auf verheimlichte Gedanken,
Die aus dem Nebel des Vergangnen schwanken.
Und jetzt belebt die Stadt sich mit Gefühl und Farben.
Es schmerzen alte, unsichtbare Narben.

Es ist, als ob die Tore sich beseelten,
In ihrem Dämmer kleine Lichter schwelten,
In deren Schein versunkene Gefährten
Sich traurig lächelnd, fragend zu mir kehrten:

"Bist du jetzt wieder hier, aus fremden Landen,
Zurück bei uns, in alten dunklen Banden?"
Ich konnte kaum die Antwort geben
Und suchte zu den Blumen und dem Parke hinzustreben.

Back in Vienna

I wander along the street, stunned.
The streets are dead, abandoned.
The years have run by already,
Youth has long since escaped me.

There rise hidden thoughts,
That stumble out of the past's fog.
And now the city reanimates itself with feeling and color.
It hurts old, invisible scars.

It's as if the gates were filled with spirit,
Little lights gleaming, twilit,
In them shine sunken companions
Who, sadly smiling, turning to me ask:

"Are you back here again, from foreign lands,
Back with us, in old dark bands?"
I could hardly give an answering remark
And headed toward the flowers and the park.

ANNA KROMMER, born in Slovakia in 1924, grew up in Berlin, where her father, a well-known graphic artist, worked for a mainstream socialist newspaper. When Nazis took over the German government in 1933, her family moved to Prague. In 1939, her father took refuge in Yugoslavia and her mother was threatened and beaten by the Gestapo. Krommer, with her mother and sister, fled to England, where she attended Guilford Technical College and the Chelsea School of Art. The family planned to return to Prague after the war, but her mother's brief visit there as an aid worker revealed that her family had been murdered during the war, and they felt uncomfortable returning. In 1946 she moved to Frankfurt to censor letters for the US military. In 1948, she moved to Palestine. In 1951, after settling her father in Boston, she returned to Israel to live in a kibbutz, where she completed her first volume of poetry. Returning to the United States in 1953, she supported herself as an au pair, then with secretarial work, finally settling in New York State, taking US citizenship in 1957.

Staub von Städten

Staub von Städten ist mir noch geblieben
von den vielen Straßen, von den Träumen.
In den Augen brennt der Staub und auf den Lippen
blieb ein Nachgeschmack mir vom Versäumen.

Wo die Sterne fielen und zerstoben,
wo der Mond die blaue Achse zog,
flimmert Staub, zieht in Wolken oben,
fällt und deckt, was abbrach und betrog.

Lange war der Weg und manchmal bitter,
langsam blieb der letzte Freund zurück;
dunkel oft, und manchmal ein Gewitter
und ein kurzes Regenbogenglück.

Staub von Städten ist mir noch geblieben;
Sternenstaub – die Poesie der Straßen,
kurze Pausen, hastig fortgetrieben
ist ein großes Netz von langen Jahren.

City Dust

Dust from cities has stuck with me
from many streets, from dreams.
The dust burns in my eyes and on my lips
remains an aftertaste of chances missed.

Where the stars fell and scattered,
where the moon drew the blue axis,
drawn up into clouds, dust flickers,
falling, covering what broke off and deceived.

The way was long and sometimes bitter,
tardily the last friend stayed back;
often dark, and sometimes thunder
and a brief rainbow-luck.

Dust from cities has stuck with me;
stardust – the poetry of the streets,
brief pauses, quickly drifted away
is a great network of long years.

MARGARETE KOLLISCH

Wiener Empfang

Ein alter Wiener, der das Büchlein las
und der mit Fleiss Vergangenes vergass,
war sehr verwundert, dass wir ungebrochen
noch besser sprachen, als er je gesprochen.

Ein junger Wiener rümpfte seine Nas':
"Es war amol, ist ein verbrauchter Gspass.
Was wissen die von unseren Problemen?
Amerika, sei stad, du kannst di schämen."

Der Alte möchte schrei'n: "Geht's aussi, rrraus!"
Der Junge schickt uns ins Versorgungshaus.
Wir aber denken uns: "Gschamster Diener!
Wir emigrierten sind die bessern Wiener."

Viennese Reception

An old Viennese man who read the little book
and, forgetting the past with diligence, took
surprise at the fact that we, unbroken,
spoke better German than he'd ever spoken.

A young Viennese man wrinkled his nose:
"That was then, now the past's at a close.
What do they know of our trouble?
Shut up America, yours are double."

The old man wants to scream: "Get out, scram!"
The young man would send us to a DP camp.
But we think to ourselves: "Oh, puh-*lease*![1]
We emigrants are better Viennese."

---

1 Literally, "faithful servant" or "at your service" ("Ihr gehorsamster Diener"), a formal greeting under the Austrian monarchy, by the twentieth century already archaic, connoting an obsequious, "brown-nosing" person, a "tool."

Freiheitsstatue im Nebel

Damals war der Himmel märchenblau,
als sie mich empfing, die große Dame.
Leuchtend zog und lockte mich ihr Name,
den ich segnete aus ferner Schau.

Der Empfang war freundlich, aber lau.
Niemals nahm sie mich in beide Arme,
daß mein kranker Mund darin erwarme. –
Heute ist sie eine Nebelfrau.

Tiefergraut in sternenlosen Nächten,
Dunst verschleiert ihre Hochgestalt.
Ist sie noch von Hoffnungsgrün umwallt?
Glüht die Fackel noch in ihrer Rechten?

Ach, sie möchte sich wie einst verfechten,
doch ihr Frauenherz ist müd' und alt.

Statue of Liberty in Fog

Before, the sky was fairy-tale blue,
as she received me, the great lady.
Brightly her name drew and lured me,
and I blessed her distant hue.

The welcome was friendly, but lukewarm.
She never took me in both arms,
so that my sick mouth might be warmed. —
Today she's a woman of fog.

Deep gray on starless nights,
haze obscures her heights.
Is she still surrounded by hopeful green, bold?
Does the torch still glow in her right hand?

Oh, she wants, as she once did, to take a stand,
but her woman's heart is tired and old.

LILI KÖRBER was born in Moscow in 1897 to a Polish mother and an Austrian father. Anti-German sentiment rose in Russia during the First World War. As the daughter of an "enemy foreigner," she was expelled from school and her father was arrested. In 1915 the family fled to Berlin. Körber studied literature, completed a doctorate, and worked as a journalist in Vienna, joining the Association of Proletarian-Revolutionary Austrian Authors and the Women's International League for Peace and Freedom. Her novel *Eine Frau erlebt den roten Alltag* (*A Woman Experiences Everyday Red Life*, 1932), describing her work in a Leningrad factory during a research trip, quickly became a best seller, though a planned second edition was quashed when Hitler took power. Passing through Berlin during a lecture tour in 1933, she took notes for her next novel, *Eine Jüdin erlebt das neue Deutschland* (*A Jewess Experiences the New Germany*, 1934). After a lecture tour through Asia, she published her fourth novel, mocking Japanese and German fascism, which caused a stir with the Japanese embassy in Vienna. In 1938, she fled to Paris to write *Eine Österreicherin erlebt den Anschluß* (*An Austrian experiences the Anschluss*, first published serially in a Zurich newspaper). Exhausted by the daily bureaucracy of refugee life in France, she planned to leave for the United States, but on Hitler's invasion of Poland, France interned all Germans between the ages of seventeen and sixty-five—including Körber's fiancé, who wasn't released until France's invasion. The couple received two visas from the US Emergency Rescue Committee, arriving in New York in 1941. A refugee aid committee gave them a room and eighty dollars. After buying a typewriter, thirty dollars remained. Körber continued write novels, most still unpublished, while working as a quality controller in a women's underwear factory, then as a nurse in New York, where she died in 1982.

Die Tragik der Taste

Es war ein Finger weiß und schlank,
der eine Taste drückte;
die Taste, die beglückte,
sie sank und sang . . .

Sank in die Tiefe weltversöhnt,
um einen Ton zu tönen,
so hellen und so schönen,
wie sie ihn nie getönt . . .

Der Finger fuhr zurück,
bemerkend mit Verzagen,
daß er die Falsche angeschlagen . . .
Er fuhr zurück . . .

The Tragedy of the Button

It was a finger slim and white,
which pressed upon a key;
the happy key
it sank and sang . . .

Sank deep, world-reconciled,
to tone a tone,
more bright and clear
than it had ever known . . .

The finger drew back,
noting with despair,
that it had hit the wrong key . . .
It drew back . . .

ERICH FRIED, born in Vienna in 1921, fled for London in 1938 after his father died as a result of a Gestapo interrogation, and worked to secure visas for members of the Young Emigrants, a group he co-founded. Later working as a commentator for the BBC, he was active in protesting the Vietnam War. An essayist and poet, he also translated authors including Shakespeare, Dylan Thomas, and Richard Wright. He died in Baden-Baden in 1988.

Angst vor der Angst

Angst was kommt
Denken vor Angst was kommt
Angst vor dem Denken was kommt
Angst vor dem Denken

Wenn es kommt
kommt es wegen der Angst
wegen der Angst vor dem Denken
die mir Angst macht

Fear of Fear

Fear of what's coming
thoughts about the fear of what's coming
fear of the thoughts of what's coming
fear of thinking

When it comes
it comes because of the fear
because of the fear of thoughts
which frighten me

Ça ira?

für Peter Weiss

Die Verbrechen von gestern
haben
die Gedenktage
an die Verbrechen von vorgestern
abgeschafft

Angesichts
der Verbrechen von heute
machen wir uns zu schaffen
mit den Gedenktagen
an die Verbrechen von gestern

Die Verbrechen von morgen
werden uns Heutige
abschaffen
ohne Gedenktage
wenn wir sie nicht verhindern

Will that do?

for Peter Weiss[1]

Yesterday's crimes
abolished
memorial days
for the day before yesterday's crimes

In the face of
the crimes of today
we busy ourselves
with memorial days
for yesterday's crimes

Tomorrow's crimes
will abolish
today's
without memorial days
if we do not prevent them

---

1 Author of *The Aesthetics of Resistance* (1974-1981).

Sources and Copyright Information

Ascher-Nash, Franzi. *Gedichte eines Lebens.* J.G. Blaschke Verlag: Darmstadt, 1976: 14.

Ausländer, Rose. "Biographische Notiz": *Aschenregen die Spur deines Namens: Gedichte und Prosa*, 1976. © S. Fischer Verlag GmbH, Frankfurt am Main, 1984. "Harlem bei Nacht," "Chinatown," "Park Avenue Party": *Amerika im austro-amerikanischen Gedicht 1938-1978.* Ed. M. Grossberg. Vienna: Bergland Verlag, 1978: 32, 31, 15. "Mit giftblauem Feuer": *Die Erde war ein atlasweißes Feld.* Frankfurt: Fischer Verlag, 1985: 157.

Becher, Ulrich. "Der schwarze Segler": *Dein Herz ist deine Heimat.* Ed. R. Felmayer. Vienna, 1955. With the kind permission of Martin Roda Becher.

Beer, Sanel. "Versagte Rettung": *Zwischen Linden und Palmen.* Vienna, 1966: 22.

Bergammer, Friedrich. "Kurzer Monolog," "Rot-Weiß-Rot": *Amerika im austro-amerikanischen Gedicht 1938-1978.* Vienna: Bergland Verlag, 1978: 43.

Berl-Lee, Maria. "Manhattan bei Nacht," "In die Catskills," "Die weißgetünchte Wohnung": *Amerika im austro-amerikanischen Gedicht*: 21, 57, 21. "Grosstadt-Einsamkeit," "Lament": *Österreichisches aus Amerika.* Ed. M. Grossberg. Vienna: Bergland Verlag, 1973: 14.

Brainin, Frederick. "Nuovo York," "42nd Street Library," "Das siebte Wien": *Das Siebte Wien.* Vienna: Verlag für Gesellschaftskritik, 1990: 40, 42, 120. "E.A. Poe-Park Terrace": *Amerika im austro-amerikanischen Gedicht 1938-1978*: 19.

Broch, Herman. "Dank für ein leeres Blatt," "Für ein Gästebuch," "*Für H.L.*," "Zum Beispiel: Walt Whitman": *Gedichte*. Zürich: Rhein-Verlag: 1953: 110, 113, 118, 119.

Buchwald, Julius. "Ich reise durch die Welt": *Österreichisches aus Amerika*: 15. "Begegnung": Julius Buchwald Collection, Leo Baeck Institute Archives.

Albert Ehrenstein. "Emigrantenlied": *Geschichte im Gedicht: Das Politische Gedicht der Austro-Amerikanischen Exilautoren des schicksaljahres 1938*. Ed. M. Grossberg. New York: Austrian Institute, 1985: 22.

Elbogen, Paul. "Ankunft": *Geschichte im Gedicht*: 29.

Farau, Alfred. "Die Rettung": *Geschichte im Gedicht*: 31.

Frey, Egon. "Wenn Dunkel droht": *Österreichisches aus Amerika*: 21.

Fried, Erich. "Angst vor der Angst": © Carl Hanser Verlag GmbH & Co. KG, Munich. "Ça ira?": *Es ist was es ist: Liebesgedichte, Angstgedichte, Zorngedicht*. Berlin: K. Wagenbach, 1983.

Fürth, Otto. "Lied des kleinen Angestellten": *Amerika im austro-amerikanischen Gedicht 1938-1978*: 48. "Wall Street, 47. Stock": *Die Schwarze Geige*. Österreische Verlagsanst: Vienna, 1968: 60.

Gong, Alfred. "USA", "Manhattan Spiritual": *Amerika im austro-amerikanischen Gedicht 1938-1978*: 6, 22.

Grossberg, Mimi. "Der amerikanische Zoll": *Kleinkunst aus Amerika: Gedichte, Chansons, Prosa von in Amerika Lebenden Autoren*. Ed. M. Grossberg. Vienna: Europäischer Verlag, 1964: 23-24. "The Listener": Exilbibliothek, Literaturhaus

Wien, N1. EB-17/1.2.1.6. "Intermezzo in der New Yorker Untergrundbahn," "Sommernacht im Ft. Tryon Park": *Amerika im austro-amerikanischen Gedicht 1938-1978*: 14, 12. "They Say": Exilbibliothek, Literaturhaus Wien, N1. EB-17/1.2.1.8. Variant English translations of "Intermezzo" and "Sommernacht" were published in by the Austrian Institute in 1986. With the kind permission of the Exilbibliothek Wien.

Grossberg, Norbert. "Central Park Hypertrophien": *Kleinkunst aus Amerika*: 25-26. "Times Square um Mitternacht": *Amerika im austro-amerikanischen Gedicht 1938-1978*: 18. "Metropolis": *Österreichisches aus Amerika*: 36.

Hartwig-Manschinger, Greta. "Ein Mann hat Heimweh": *Kleinkunst aus Amerika*: 43.

Kollisch, Margarete. "New York Sky-Line," "Freiheitsstatue im Nebel": *Frauen Schreiben im Exil: Zum Werk der nach Amerika emigrierten Lyrikerinnen Margarete Kollisch, Ilse Blumenthal-Weiss, Vera Lachmann*. Frankfurt: Peter Lang, 1988: 190. "Mai in der Wall Street": *Kleinkunst aus Amerika*: 51. "Wiener Empfang": *Geschichte im Gedicht*: 88. © M.E. Grenander Department of Special Collections & Archives, University of Albany.

Körber, Lili. "Die Tragik der Taste": *Kleinkunst aus Amerika*: 62.

Kramer, Theodor. "Wiedersehen mit der Heimat": *Gesammelte Gedichte*, vol. 3. Ed. E. Chvojka. Vienna: Zsolnay Verlag: 590.

Krommer, Anna. "Staub von Städten": *Staub von Städten: Ausgewählte Gedichte*. Verlag der Theodor Kramer Gesellschaft, 1995: 77.

Roden, Max. "Erste Tage im Häusergebirge," "Hirt ohne Herde," "Sekundenballade," "Häuser meiner Heimat," "Fremde du, o

Heimat du," "In Wien 1956," "Sterben auch": *Tod und Mond und Glas.* Vienna: Bergland Verlag, 1959: 19, 16, 18, 48-49, 26, 49, 14-15.

Schick, Alfred. "Wieder in Wien": *Geschichte im Gedicht*: 83.

Tanzer, Francisco. "Später einmal": *Der Österreicher in mir: Leben und Werk.* Ed. D. Strigl. Vienna: Edition Atelier, 2006: 196. With the kind permission of Maria C. Tanzer.

Urzidil, Gertrude. "Grosses Geschick": *Geschichte im Gedicht*: 34. "Fragen eines Kindes," "Zinshaus tief in Queens": *Amerika im austro-amerikanischen Gedicht 1938-1978*: 25.

Viertel, Berthold. "Auswanderer," "Gekritzel auf der Rückseite eines Reisepasses," "Ohne Decke, ohne Kohlen: *Das graue Tuch.* Ed. K. Kaiser. Vienna: Verlag für Gesellschaftskritik, 1994: 172, 173, 315.

Waldinger, Ernst. "Ein Pferd in der 47. Straße," "Der Wolkenkratzer": *Zwischen Hudson und Donau.* Vienna, Bergland Verlag, 1958: 9-10, 6-8. "Nachts am Hudson": *Die Kühlen Bauernstuben.* New York: Aurora Verlag, 1946: 89. "© Otto Müller Verlag.

Weiskopf, Franz Carl. "Eine Bibliothek in New York": *Gesammelte Werke*, vol. 8. Berlin: Dietz Verlag, 1960: 21-23.

Zernatto, Guido. "Aus tausend Quellen," "Dieser Wind der fremden Kontinente": *Die Sonnenuhr.* Salzburg: Otto Müller Verlag, 1961: 31, 127.

Zweig, Friderike Maria. "Traum im Winter": *Geschichte im Gedicht*: 49.

Zweig, Stefan. "Hymnus an die Reise," "Die ferne Landschaft," "Abendliche Flucht": *Silberne Saiten*. Ed. R. Friedenthal. Frankfurt: Fischer Verlag, 1966: 95, 103-04, 109. © S. Fischer Verlag. "Der Rhythmus von New York": *Auf Reisen: Feuilltons und Berichte*. Frankfurt: Fischer Verlag, 1987: 135-43. "Der verlorene Himmel": *Fahrten: Landschaften und Städte*. Leipzig: E.P. Tal & Co., 1919: 118-22.

Secondary Sources

Abish, Walter. *Double Vision*. New York: Alfred A. Knopf, 2004.

Adunka Evelyn, Primavera Driesen-Gruber and Simon Usaty with Fritz Hausjell and Irene Nawrocka, eds. *Exilforschung: Österreich: Leistungen, Defizite & Perspektiven* (Exilforschung heute vol. 4). Vienna: Mandelbaum Verlag, 2018.

Arendt, Hannah. "We Refugees." *Menorah Journal* 31.1 (1943): 69-77.

Bischof, Günter and Hannes Richter. *Towards the American Century: Austrians in the United States*. New Orleans: University of New Orleans Press, 2019.

Bischof, Günter. "Austria's Loss - America's Gain: *Finis Austriae* - The "Anschluss" and the Expulsion/Migration of Jewish Austrians to the U.S.," in: idem, *Relationships/Beziehungsgeschichten: Austria and the United States in the Twentieth Century* (TRANSATLANTICA 4). Innsbruck: StudienVerlag 2014.

————. "'Busy with Refugee Work': Joseph Buttinger, Muriel Gardiner, and the Saving of Austrian Refugees, 1940–1941," in: Claudia Kuretsidis-Haider and Christine Schindler im Auftrag des Dokumentationsarchivs des österreichischen Widerstandes und der Zentralen österreichischen Foschungsstelle Nachkriegsjustiz, ed. *Zeithistoriker – Archivar – Aufklärer: Festschrift für Winfried R. Garscha*. Vienna 2017. 115-26.

————. "Exile Studies in Austria," in Günter Bischof and David M. Wineroither, eds, *Democracy in Austria* (Contemporary Austrian Studies 28. (New Orleans-Innsbruck: UNO Press/ Innsbruck University Press, 2019. 309-18.

Brude-Firnau, Gisela. "Herman Broch." *Deutschsprachige Exilliteratur seit 1933*. Band 2, Teil 3: New York. Ed. J.M. Spalek and J. Strelka. Bern: Francke Verlag, 1989. 132-60.

Bushell, Anthony. "Many Happy Returns? Attitudes to Exile in Austria's Literary and Cultural Journals in the early Post-war Years." *"Immortal Austria?" Austrians in Exile in Britain*. Ed. C. Brinson, R. Dove and J. Taylor. Amsterdam and New York: Rodopi, 2007. 197-209.

Csokor, Franz Theodor. *Auch heute noch nicht an Land: Briefe und Gedichte aus dem Exil*. Ed. Franz Richard Reiter. Vienna: Ephelant Verlag, 1993.

Drekonja, Otmar M. "Guido Zernatto." *Deutschsprachige Exilliteratur seit 1933*. Band 3, Teil 3: New York. Ed. J.M. Spalek and J. Strelka. Bern: Francke Verlag, 1989. 997-1009.

Faulhaber, Uwe. "Albert Ehrenstein." *Deutschsprachige Exilliteratur seit 1933*. Band 2, Teil 3: New York. Ed. J.M. Spalek and J. Strelka. Bern: Francke Verlag, 1989. 186-93.

Flügge Manfred. *Stadt ohne Seele: Wien 1938*. Berlin: Aufbau Verlag, 2018.

Fried, Erich. *100 Gedichte ohne Vaterland*. 1978. Frankfurt: Fischer Taschenbuch Verlag, 1993.

Goldner, Franz. *Die Österreichische Emigration 1938 bis 1945*. Vienna: Verlag Harold, 1977.

Haacker, Christoph. "Anna Krommer." *Deutschsprachige Exilliteratur seit 1933*. Band 3, Teil 3: USA. Ed. J.M. Spalek, K. Feilchenfedt and S.H. Hawrylchak. Munich: K.G. Saur Verlag, 2002. 48-94.

Hampe, Kurt. "Einleitende Worte." *Kleinkunst aus Amerika: Gedichte, Chanson, Prosa von in Amerika lebenden Autoren*. Ed. M. Grossberg. Vienna: Europäischer Verlag, 1964. 3.

Harshav, Benjamin and Barbara. *AmericanYiddish Poetry:A Bilingual Anthology*. Berkeley: U of California P, 1986.

Heilbut, Anthony. *Exiled in Paradise: German Refugee Artists and Intellectuals in America, from the 1930s to the Present*. New York: Viking, 1983.

Hertling, Viktoria. "Lili Körber." *Deutschsprachige Exilliteratur seit 1933*. Band 2, Teil 3: New York. Ed. J.M. Spalek, K. Feilchenfedt and S.H. Hawrylchak. Munich: K.G. Saur Verlag, 1989. 448-60.

Herz-Kestranek, Miguel, Konstantin Kaiser and Daniela Stringl. "Einleitung." *In welcher Sprache träumen Sie? Österreichische Exillyrik*. Vienna: Theodor Kramer Gesellschaft, 2007.

Hilberg, Raul. *The Politics of Memory: The Journey of a Holocaust Historian*. Chicago: Ivan R. Dee, 1996.

Jelinek, Gerhard. *Nachrichten aus dem 4. Reich*. Salzburg: Ecowin Verlag, 2008.

Kauf, Robert. "Ernst Waldinger." *Deutschsprachige Exilliteratur seit 1933*. Band 2, Teil 2: New York. Ed. J.M. Spalek and J. Strelka. Bern: Francke Verlag, 1989. 985-96.

Limberg, Margarete and Hubert Rübsaat, eds. *Nach dem "Anschluss"... Berichte österreichischer EmigrantInnen aus dem Archiv der Harvard University*. Vienna: Mandelbaum, 2013.

Macris, Ursula. "Otto Fürth." *Deutschsprachige Exilliteratur seit 1933.* Band 3, Teil 1: USA. Ed. J.M. Spalek, K. Feilchenfedt and S.H. Hawrylchak. Munich: K.G. Saur Verlag, 2000. 131-41.

Putz, Kerstin, "Improvised Lives: Günther Anders's American Exile." *Quiet Invaders Revisited: Biographies of Twentieth Century Immigrants to the United States.* Ed. Günter Bischof. Innsbruck: Studien Verlag, 2017. 231-42.

Reinhardt, Max. "Resignation: 1943." Ed. H. Fetting. *Max Reinhardt Schriften: Briefe, Aufsätze, Interviews, Gespräche, Auszüge aus Regiebüchern.* Berlin: Henschelverlag Kunst und Gesellschaft, 1974. 253-54.

Roden, Max. "In Wien 1958." *Tod und Mond und Glas.* Vienna: Bergland Verlag, 1959. 50.

Romero, Christiane Zehl. "Franz Carl Weiskopf." *Deutschsprachige Exilliteratur seit 1933.* Band 3, Teil 5: USA. Ed. J.M. Spalek, K. Feilchenfedt and S.H. Hawrylchak. Munich: K.G. Saur Verlag, 2005. 240-70.

"Roundtable on Manfred Flügge's *Stadt Ohne Seele*." In Günter Bischof and David M. Wineroither, eds. *Democracy in Austria* (Contemporary Austrian Studies 28). New Orleans-Innsbruck: UNO Press/Innsbruck University Press, 2019. 275-305.

Schönwiese, Ernst. "Friedrich Bergammer." *Deutschsprachige Exilliteratur seit 1933.* Band 2, Teil 3: New York. Ed. J.M. Spalek and J. Strelka. Bern: Francke Verlag, 1989. 97-108.

Segal, Lore. *Other People's Houses.* 1964. New York and London: The New Press, 1990.

————. *Her First American.* 1985. New York and London: The New Press, 2004.

Spaulding, E. Wilder. *The Quiet Invaders: The Story of the Austrian Impact Upon America.* Vienna: Österreichischer Bundesverlag für Unterricht, Wissenschaft und Kunst, 1968.

Strelka, Joseph P. "Alfred Gong." *Deutschsprachige Exilliteratur seit 1933.* Band 2, Teil 3: New York. Ed. J.M. Spalek, K. Feilchenfedt and S.H. Hawrylchak. Munich: K.G. Saur Verlag, 1989. 260-69.

Strobl, Philipp. "Thinking Cosmopolitan or How Joseph Became Joe Buttinger." In Günter Bischof, Fritz Plasser and Eva Maltschnig, eds. *Austrian Lives* (Contemporary Austrian Studies 21). New Orleans/Innsbruck: UNO Press/Innsbruck University Press, 2012. 92-122.

Troller, Georg Stefan. *Wohin und zurück: Die Axel-Corti-Trilogie.* Vienna: Theodor Kramer Gesellschaft, 2009.

————. "Sprache in der Emigration." *Mit meiner Schreibmaschine: Geschichten und Begegnungen.* Hürth bei Köln: Edition Memoria, 2014. 49-79.

Weiskopf, Franz Carl. "Sprache im Exil." *Über Literatur und Sprach: Literarische Streifzüge Verteidigung der Deutschen Sprache.* Berlin: Dietz Verlag, 1960. 483-93.

Weissenberger, Klaus. "Rose Ausländer." *Deutschsprachige Exilliteratur seit 1933.* Band 2, Teil 3: New York. Ed. J.M. Spalek, K. Feilchenfedt and S.H. Hawrylchak. Munich: K.G. Saur Verlag, 1989. 9-23.

Wright, Richard. "High Tide in Harlem: Joe Louis as a Symbol of Freedom." *Weekly Masses* (5 July 1938): 18-20.

Zeller, Nancy Anne McClure. "Ulrich Becher." Trans. B.O. Strelka. *Deutschsprachige Exilliteratur seit 1933*. Band 2, Teil 3: New York. Ed. J.M. Spalek and J. Strelka. Bern: Francke Verlag, 1989. 51-67.